HOW TO INVEST FOR TEENS

How to Build Your First Profitable Portfolio in 7 Days—No Adult Required and Zero Experience Needed

Maxi Tonkins

Published by Authors Crib

www.AuthorsCrib.com

Formatted using Lacuna

PREFACE

Let's be real: most books about money are boring.

They're filled with confusing jargon, written for people who already own a yacht, and engineered to make you feel like you need an economics degree just to understand what a stock is. If you picked up this book, you probably already know the crucial truth: waiting until you are thirty to start investing is basically just throwing money away.

You're not here to wait. You're smart, you're curious, and you are ready to make your money work harder than you do. That's exactly what this guide is for. We are not going to talk about ancient history or abstract financial theories. We are here to talk about getting started, right now.

Over the next seven days, we are going to cut through the noise, skip the confusing adult lectures, and give you the straightforward, witty, and easy-to-follow plan you need to launch your very first portfolio. We will walk step-by-step through setting up your accounts, making your first purchases, and understanding exactly what you own. No parental supervision required (well, mostly).

Get ready to ditch the complicated language and embrace real financial confidence. You are about to trade confusion for capital. Your future self is going to thank you. Let's get to work.

TABLE OF CONTENTS

INTRODUCTION

THE 'ADULT' SUPERPOWER THEY NEVER TAUGHT YOU IN SCHOOL (AND HOW TO UNLOCK IT TODAY)

If you've ever felt like the economy is a massive, impenetrable game where all the rules are hidden and only the super-rich know the cheat codes, you're right. But you're also wrong. The rules aren't hidden—they are simply obscured by unnecessary jargon and the greatest lie ever told about wealth creation: that it's only for "adults."

Welcome to the real game of wealth creation, and congratulations on picking up the master playbook.

Forget every get-rich-quick promise you've seen online. This book won't teach you how to trade meme stocks or double your money overnight. This book will teach you how to turn spare cash—the money you earn from a summer job, allowance, or birthday gifts—into future financial freedom. Investing is the true superpower they never taught you in history, math, or driver's ed, and it is the only reliable path to building lasting wealth.

For too long, the financial world has operated like an exclusive club, handing out membership only after you graduate college, get a "real job," and are perhaps already deep in debt. We are dismantling that barrier right now. Investing is not reserved for those who wear suits or read the Wall Street

Journal at 6 a.m. It is a fundamental skill, and the younger you unlock it, the faster and farther you will go.

The biggest advantage you possess right now isn't intelligence, grit, or a giant bank account; it is time.

We are going to introduce you to the ultimate financial cheat code: compounding. Compounding is the magical concept where your earnings start generating their own earnings, creating a financial snowball that gets bigger and faster the longer it rolls. Starting at 16, 17, or 18 means you have an extra decade—maybe two—of compounding power compared to your peers who wait until their twenties or thirties. This time advantage is mathematically worth hundreds of thousands of dollars, maybe even millions. It is literally the most valuable asset you have, and you must deploy it immediately.

This book is structured as a practical, seven-day challenge. We are going to cut through the confusion, skip the confusing lectures, and move straight to action.

In the next seven days, we will cover:

Day 1-2: Mindset and Resources. We define your goals and show you how to find money in your current cash flow to fund your first investment.

Day 3-4: The Launchpad. We secure the perfect, teen-friendly, legal account setup and introduce you to the core investment creatures—the stocks and funds that will do the heavy lifting for you.

Day 5-7: Execution and Automation. We teach you how to research investments like a pro, place your first trades, and set up an automated system so your money grows without you constantly lifting a finger.

By the end of this guide, the entire world of finance—which currently might look like a dark, confusing maze—will transform into a clear, bright path leading directly to your goals, whether that's a new gaming rig, college tuition, or true independence.

Prepare to feel confident, capable, and ready to make your money matter. The power is yours. Let's unlock it.

CHAPTER ONE

THE ULTIMATE CHEAT CODE: WHY STARTING AT 16 TRUMPS STARTING AT 30 (THE $500,000 TIME ADVANTAGE)

YOU ARE CURRENTLY STANDING AT A UNIQUE CROSSROADS IN LIFE, one that almost every adult wishes they could return to. You might feel like you're powerless because you don't have a six-figure salary or a corner office, but the truth is, you possess the single most valuable asset in finance: Time.

Think of time as an invisible $500,000 check handed to you simply for starting young.

Most people wait until they have "enough money" or "enough experience" to begin investing, usually in their late 20s or 30s. They spend those critical early years focused on consuming, believing investing is something for retirement or their parents' generation. By reading this book now, you are effectively taking a shortcut past those decades of procrastination, activating the most powerful cheat code in financial history: compounding interest.

This chapter isn't about picking stocks yet; it's about upgrading your brain's operating system. We're going to dismantle the limiting beliefs that keep most people poor, understand the unstoppable mathematical engine that makes money grow, and set the coordinates for your future financial freedom. Get ready to stop being just a consumer and start becoming an owner.

REVEALED: The One Secret Mindset Shift That Separates Consumers From Millionaires

If you look around your room right now, you can probably identify dozens of things you purchased: new sneakers, a streaming subscription, the latest video game, snacks. You are a consumer. You paid cash to own these items, and the moment you used them, they began to lose value.

There is nothing wrong with being a consumer—it's necessary—but if you want to build wealth, you must recognize the fundamental difference between consumption and ownership.

The secret mindset shift that separates those who struggle with money from those who build generational wealth is simple: Stop renting your time and start owning assets.

Saving vs. Investing: Why Your Money Needs a Job

Many people confuse saving with investing. Let's clarify:

Saving is when you take cash and put it somewhere safe, like under your mattress or in a basic savings account. The money doesn't grow. In fact, due to inflation—the sneaky economic force that makes everything more expensive every year—your saved money actually loses buying power over time. A dollar saved today buys less next year. Saving is essential for short-term goals (like an emergency fund or buying a concert ticket), but it's a terrible strategy for building long-term wealth.

Investing is when you take cash and use it to buy an asset that has the potential to produce more cash. When you buy a stock in a company, you are literally buying a tiny piece of that company. You become an owner. When that company makes a profit, you, the owner, benefit.

Think about the products you use every single day: your iPhone, your Spotify subscription, your favorite brand of energy drink. When you buy these things, you transfer your money to the corporation. But when you buy stock in Apple, Spotify, or Coca-Cola, you are transforming yourself from a mere customer into a business partner. Every time another customer buys a product from a company you own, your investment potentially increases in value.

This is the Investor Mindset. It's about delayed gratification and strategic patience. It's choosing to put $50 toward owning a piece of the next big tech company instead of blowing $50 on fast food or a new skin in a game. That small shift, executed consistently, is the engine of millionaire creation. You are programming your money to work harder than you do.

THE SNOWBALL EFFECT: HOW YOUR FIRST $100 CAN TURN INTO $10,000 WHILE YOU SLEEP

If you only learn one financial concept in this book, let it be Compounding Interest.

Albert Einstein reportedly called compounding the eighth wonder of the world. It's the closest thing to real-life magic you will ever experience, and it is entirely dependent on time.

What is Compounding?

It is earning returns not only on the money you invested (the principal) but also on the returns you've already earned.

Imagine a small snowball at the top of a massive hill. That small snowball is your first investment ($100). As it rolls down, it picks up snow (returns). In the second rotation, it is now larger, so it picks up even more snow. By the time it reaches the bottom of the hill, it's a giant, unstoppable boulder.

In finance, the hill is time. The longer the snowball rolls, the more returns it earns on its returns.

Let's look at the numbers—because this is the mathematical proof of your $500,000 advantage. We will assume both investors earn an average historical return of 8% per year, which is standard for the stock market over the long run.

Scenario 1: The Teen Investor (You)

Age: 16

Contribution: $200 per month

Duration of Contribution: 10 years (ages 16-26)

Total Cash Contributed: $24,000

Stops Contributing at 26: The money sits invested, untouched, until age 65.

Scenario 2: The Waiter (The 30-Year-Old)

Age: 30

Contribution: $200 per month

Duration of Contribution: 35 years (ages 30-65)

Total Cash Contributed: $84,000

Look at the results when both investors turn 65:

Investor	**Age Started**	**Total Contributed**	**Final Value at Age 65 (8% Return)**
You (Started at 16)	16	$24,000	$797,000
The Waiter (Started at 30)	30	$84,000	$437,000

This comparison is jaw-dropping. The teen investor (You) contributed $60,000 less cash but ended up with over $360,000 more wealth than the adult who waited 14 years longer to start.

The difference is purely the power of the compounding snowball. Your $24,000 had an extra 14 years of uninterrupted growth, where your initial returns started earning their own returns, exponentially growing your wealth while you were still in high school or college.

This is why starting early is the ultimate cheat code: it allows a small, consistent contribution to massively outperform a larger, later contribution. Time is your best friend.

——★-★-★——

EXPOSED: THE 3 BIGGEST LIES THAT KEEP 99% OF TEENS FROM INVESTING (HINT: YOU DON'T NEED $1,000 OR A DEGREE)

If investing is so simple and the math is so clear, why aren't all teens investing? Because they've been fed a set of persistent lies perpetuated by Hollywood movies and confusing financial news. Let's dismantle the three most damaging myths right now.

LIE #1: I NEED THOUSANDS OF DOLLARS TO START

This might have been true in 1985, but it is pure fiction today. In the past, you often needed enough cash to buy at least one full share of a stock, and shares of companies like Amazon or Google can cost hundreds or even thousands of dollars.

The Truth: Thanks to modern brokerage platforms (which we will cover in Chapter 3), you can now buy Fractional Shares. This means if you only have $10, you can buy 0.01 shares of Google. If you have $25, you can spread that money across ten different companies.

Starting with $10 per week is infinitely better than waiting until you have $1,000 to invest. Remember the compounding snowball—consistency and time beat initial size every single time. Your goal right now is to establish the habit of investing, not to become a sudden millionaire.

LIE #2: I NEED AN ECONOMICS DEGREE OR TO BE A FINANCE GENIUS

The image of a sweaty, shouting stockbroker on Wall Street is what most people associate with investing. This perception leads young people to believe they need to be mathematical prodigies who spend eight hours a day analyzing complex financial statements.

The Truth: The single most effective and reliable strategy for long-term wealth building—the strategy favored by billionaires like Warren Buffett—is incredibly boring and simple: Invest consistently in low-cost index funds.

Index funds (which we'll detail in Chapter 4) simply track the performance of the overall market, like the S&P 500. When you buy an index fund, you are buying a tiny slice of the 500 largest companies in the United States. You don't need to predict which one will win; you just bet on the entire American economy.

This strategy requires zero financial expertise. It requires discipline, patience, and the ability to click the "Buy" button every month. If you can pass a basic algebra class, you are already overqualified for the math required to succeed in long-term investing.

LIE #3: I NEED MY PARENTS' PERMISSION FOR EVERY STEP

Because you are a minor (under 18 or 21, depending on the state), you cannot legally sign a contract to open a brokerage account on your own. This fact often leads teens to believe they are shut out of the investment world entirely.

The Truth: You need a Custodial Account, specifically a UTMA or UGMA account (Uniform Transfers to Minors Act / Uniform Gifts to Minors Act).

In simple terms, an adult (usually a parent or guardian, known as the custodian) opens the account for you. They legally manage the account until you reach the age of majority (usually 18 or 21). However, the money legally belongs to you, the minor.

While you need an adult to handle the initial paperwork and legal oversight, they are simply the gateway. You are the beneficial owner, and you can, and absolutely should, be the one making the investment decisions and learning how to navigate the markets. This book provides the playbook to make informed decisions so your parents can confidently sign the papers and let you take the lead on the investment choices.

—★–★–★—

THE INVESTOR'S WISH LIST: HOW TO FUND THAT GAMING PC, COLLEGE, OR FUTURE MANSION (THE GOAL-SETTING MECHANISM)

Before you start clicking "Buy," you need a destination. Investing without goals is like driving without GPS—you'll burn fuel and get nowhere specific.

Goal setting is the foundation of turning that difficult concept of "delayed gratification" into an achievable reality. Delayed gratification isn't about denying yourself pleasure forever; it's about deferring a small, immediate pleasure (like a $20 splurge on a game) for a much larger, more meaningful future reward (like funding a gap year abroad).

Your financial goals will directly dictate how you invest—specifically, how much risk you should take. We categorize goals based on time horizons:

1. SHORT-TERM GOALS (1-3 YEARS):

These are things you want soon, like buying a high-end gaming PC, funding a car down payment, or traveling after graduation. Since the time horizon is short, your money doesn't have enough time to recover from a major market downturn.

Strategy: Keep this money safe. Use high-yield savings accounts or Certificates of Deposit (CDs). Do not invest this money in the volatile stock market.

2. MEDIUM-TERM GOALS (3-10 YEARS):

This usually centers on college tuition, paying for certifications, or saving up for the initial deposit on a property. Since you have a few years, your money can afford moderate risk, but still needs a relatively stable path.

Strategy: A mix of safety and growth. Perhaps 50% conservative investments (like bonds, detailed in Chapter 4) and 50% broad market index funds.

3. LONG-TERM GOALS (10+ YEARS):

This is the big one: financial independence, retirement, and massive wealth accumulation. Because you have decades for the compounding effect to work, you have an incredible capacity for risk. Market dips are irrelevant over this time frame.

Strategy: Be aggressive. 80% to 100% in growth-focused investments (stocks and low-cost index funds). This is where the magic of compounding delivers its highest returns.

YOUR FIRST ASSIGNMENT: WRITE DOWN YOUR GOALS

GRAB A PEN AND PAPER OR OPEN A NOTE ON YOUR PHONE. WRITE down one goal for each category and assign a dollar amount and a timeline.

Example:

Short-Term: $1,500 for a new graphics card by July 2026.

Medium-Term: $15,000 for college/travel fund by August 2030.

Long-Term: Financial independence by age 45 (Goal: $1,000,000).

Now, every time you're about to spend money impulsively, you can run a quick cost-benefit analysis: Does this $20 soda and snack make me happier than taking a tiny step closer to that $15,000 college fund?

By linking every investment decision to a powerful, concrete goal, you transform the abstract idea of "getting rich someday" into an actionable, inspiring plan. You've now mastered the mindset. In the next chapter, we put that mindset to work by figuring out exactly where your initial investment money is going to come from.

—★–★–★—

REVEALED: THE ONE SECRET MINDSET SHIFT THAT SEPARATES CONSUMERS FROM MILLIONAIRES

LET'S START WITH A BRUTAL TRUTH: YOU HAVE BEEN TRAINED YOUR whole life to be an amazing consumer.

Think about it. From the moment you saw your first commercial for a toy or watched a YouTuber endorse a gadget, your brain has been wired to spend money. And you're good at it! When you buy the newest sneakers, stream the latest series, or grab a fast-food meal, you are fulfilling your role as the ideal consumer. You hand over your hard-earned cash, and those dollars disappear forever.

In this classic dynamic, you are always the one paying.

The fundamental, non-negotiable mindset shift that separates those who struggle financially from those who build serious wealth is this: You must transition from being primarily a Consumer to being primarily an Owner.

What does that look like in practice?

The Consumer Mindset sees money as something to be spent, or at best, something to be saved for short-term purchases. They think, "I have $500, I will keep it in my checking account so I can buy those concert tickets later."

The Owner Mindset sees money as Resource Units that must be immediately assigned a job: generating more Resource Units. They think, "I have $500, I will put $400 into an investment account so it can buy me concert tickets every year using the profit it generates."

The difference isn't just in how you spend; it's in how you view the money you don't spend.

The Myth of the Mattress Money

When you get paid for a gig or receive a generous birthday gift, the most common beginner instinct is to save the cash. You might stuff it into a piggy bank, leave it sitting in a low-interest savings account, or, heaven forbid, put it under your mattress.

This strategy is a guaranteed path to losing money.

Wait, what? How can you lose money if you haven't spent it?

Meet your financial enemy: Inflation.

Inflation is the sneaky little thief that constantly diminishes the buying power of your money. It means that the cost of everything—from a gallon of milk to the newest iPhone—goes up over time. If you keep $1,000 in cash for ten years, it still says $1,000, but because prices rose 3% every year, that thousand dollars now buys significantly less than it did a decade ago. It has shrunk in value, even though the number hasn't changed. Your savings account might give you 0.1% interest, which is like trying to put out a forest fire with a water pistol.

The Consumer saves cash and watches its value erode.

The Owner buys assets and watches their value grow faster than inflation.

The Key to the Kingdom: Ownership

When you invest, you are essentially buying a tiny slice of ownership in a real, functioning company. You are not just buying the newest iPhone; you are buying a tiny part of Apple, Inc.

This is the engine of wealth creation. When you buy a stock or a fund, you are doing three powerful things:

1. You are putting your money to work. Instead of sitting stagnant, your money is now actively funding innovation, production, and marketing at companies that make real profits.

2. You benefit from growth. If Apple sells more iPhones and their profit goes up, the value of the stock you own increases. Your money makes more money, and you haven't lifted a finger.

3. You get paid for being the boss. Many mature companies pay out a portion of their profits directly to owners in the form of dividends. This is essentially free cash flow that rolls into your account, and you can reinvest it to buy more ownership.

The consumer gives their money away and gets a product in return. The owner gives their money away (temporarily, in exchange for a stock) and gets a slice of future profits and growth in return.

This shift—from thinking of yourself as a user of things to a part-owner of the world's most successful businesses—is the single most important secret that high-net-worth individuals understood early on. Now, you do too. Everything in this guide is designed to help you execute this secret effectively.

—★-★-★—

THE SNOWBALL EFFECT: HOW YOUR FIRST $100 CAN TURN INTO $10,000 WHILE YOU SLEEP

If you've heard any financial advice that sounds like magic, it was probably about compounding interest. It's not magic, but it is the single most powerful tool in the universe of money. In fact, Albert Einstein is sometimes quoted as calling compounding the "eighth wonder of the world."

Here is the secret: Compounding is simply earning returns on your returns.

Think of it like a tiny, perfectly round snowball you place at the very top of a long, snowy hill.

When you start, the snowball (your initial investment, maybe $100) is small. As it rolls down, it collects snow (that snow represents the interest or returns you earn). In the beginning, the growth is slow, barely noticeable. After the first 100 feet, your snowball is maybe twice its original size.

But here is where the physics of compounding kick in: The next 100 feet are easier because the snowball is now rolling with a larger surface area. It collects snow faster. By the time it hits the bottom of the hill, it's not just big; it's massive, perhaps taller than you are.

Crucially, it didn't just grow by adding new snow; it grew because the snow it collected earlier started collecting even more snow. Your money is doing the same thing. You earn interest on your original deposit, and then you earn interest on that interest. You put in $100, you earn $10, and now your account is earning money on $110, not just $100. That's the snowball effect, and time is the length of the hill.

The beautiful reality of compounding is that the size of your initial investment matters far less than the amount of time you give that snowball to roll.

The time advantage you possess right now, as a young investor, is literally worth hundreds of thousands of dollars. Let's prove it.

THE $500,000 DIFFERENCE: WHY TEN YEARS MATTERS

IMAGINE TWO FRIENDS, BOTH AIMING TO RETIRE AT 65. BOTH ARE smart, disciplined, and commit to investing $200 every month (or $2,400 per year). We will assume an average historical return of 10%—which is typical for a long-term investment in the stock market.

Investor A: The 16-Year-Old Early Bird

Starts investing at age 16.

Contributes $200 per month until age 65 (49 years of compounding).

Total money contributed: $117,600.

Final Nest Egg at 65: Approximately $2,875,000.

Investor B: The 26-Year-Old Late Bloomer

Starts investing at age 26.

Contributes $200 per month until age 65 (39 years of compounding).

Total money contributed: $93,600.

Final Nest Egg at 65: Approximately $1,090,000.

Look closely at the numbers. Investor A, the 16-year-old, contributed only $24,000 more in their lifetime (just $200 a month for 10 extra years). But because they gave their money ten additional years to roll down the compounding hill, they finished with $1,785,000 more than their friend who waited a single decade.

If we were to draw a chart, the difference would look like a hockey stick:

1. Ages 16-26: Investor A's line creeps up slowly. It's earning, but the growth is small. Investor B is flat.

2. Ages 26-45: Both lines start moving upward, but Investor A's line is visibly higher.

3. Ages 45-65: Investor A's line shoots up nearly vertically. The gap between the two investors becomes a chasm. This is where the compounding really accelerates, and Investor A is earning hundreds of thousands of dollars simply on the interest their early investments generated.

This is the central pillar of why starting young is the ultimate cheat code. You don't need a giant pile of cash; you need time. Your first $100, invested today, will likely be worth far more at age 65 than the $1,000 you invest when you're 40, because that initial $100 has nearly half a century to compound.

Your mission is to get that tiny snowball rolling now, and then feed it consistently. The universe will handle the exponential growth.

—★-★-★—

EXPOSED: THE 3 BIGGEST LIES THAT KEEP 99% OF TEENS FROM INVESTING (HINT: YOU DON'T NEED $1,000 OR A DEGREE)

If you've heard that investing is too complicated, too expensive, or too risky for a teenager, you've been listening to the old, outdated rules of finance. These are the three biggest myths perpetuated by people who either don't invest themselves or who started 30 years ago when the rules were totally different.

It's time to expose them.

LIE #1: YOU NEED THOUSANDS OF DOLLARS TO START

THIS IS PERHAPS THE MOST PERSISTENT AND FRUSTRATING LIE OUT there. Generations ago, if you wanted to buy a single share of a major company like Amazon or Google, you might need hundreds or even thousands of dollars. If you were starting out with $50 from mowing lawns, you were completely locked out.

The Reality: You can start with $5.

The technology that powers your brokerage account has evolved faster than Wall Street's reputation. Today, the game-changing feature for teen investors is the invention of fractional shares.

What is a fractional share? It's exactly what it sounds like: a small slice of a very expensive stock. Instead of needing $3,000 for one full share of Stock X, you can tell your brokerage, "I want to buy $10 worth of Stock X." They will give you 0.0033 shares. You still get the growth, and your $10 is now invested in a top-tier company.

Since most major, teen-friendly brokerages (which we'll cover in Chapter 3) offer fractional shares and have zero account minimums, the barrier to entry is completely gone. If you have enough money for a large pizza, you have enough money to start investing. Your focus should be on consistency, not capital size.

LIE #2: YOU NEED TO BE A FINANCE GENIUS (OR HAVE A COLLEGE DEGREE)

MOVIES AND TV SHOWS LOVE TO PORTRAY INVESTORS AS HYPER-CAFfeinated math wizards shouting complex jargon across a trading floor. This imagery is designed to intimidate and make you feel like unless you understand the difference between EBITDA and CAPEX, you shouldn't even bother.

The Reality: Success in investing requires discipline and time, not genius.

The fundamental truth of successful investing is that complexity often kills returns. The simplest, most effective strategy—the one championed by billionaire legends like Warren Buffett—is often the most boring: buying broad index funds and holding them for decades.

You do not need to read the daily news or memorize the price-to-earnings (P/E) ratio of every stock. You simply need to understand a few core concepts (like the magic of compounding, which we discussed earlier) and trust the long-term growth of the global economy.

In fact, being an outsider is often an advantage. Since you aren't bogged down in complicated jargon, you can focus on the basics:

1. Does the company make money?
2. Will people still be using this product in 10 years?
3. Is this a necessary technology?

You, as a young, tech-savvy consumer, have an advantage over 50-year-old financial analysts because you understand current trends—the apps, the gaming companies, the social media platforms—that are defining the future. Don't underestimate your consumer knowledge; it's a powerful research tool (as we'll discuss in Chapter 5).

LIE #3: YOU NEED YOUR PARENTS' PERMISSION FOR EVERY SINGLE MOVE

WHILE YOU ARE A MINOR, THE LAW REQUIRES THAT AN ADULT ACT AS the custodian (manager) of your account. This is designed to protect you, but many teens misunderstand this rule to mean that they have zero control over their money and their parents must be consulted before every $25 purchase.

The Reality: The account is yours, and you are the decision-maker.

When you open a custodial account (like a UGMA or UTMA, which we detail later), the money legally belongs to you, the minor. The adult is simply the steward or manager until you turn 18 (or 21, depending on the state).

The best part about modern custodial accounts is that they are built for education. Many major brokerages allow the teen to download the app, perform the research, and place the trades independently. The custodian (parent or guardian) usually only needs to approve the initial account setup and perhaps the funding transfer.

Think of it like driving. Your parent might be in the passenger seat, required by law to be there, but you are the one behind the wheel navigating the route. Your custodian is there for oversight, not micro-management.

By starting now, you demonstrate financial maturity and responsibility, which usually leads to greater trust and autonomy from your parents regarding your investment decisions. The key is to show you've done your homework. And reading this book is the first step in proving that.

THE INVESTOR'S WISH LIST: HOW TO FUND THAT GAMING PC, COLLEGE, OR FUTURE MANSION (THE GOAL-SETTING MECHANISM)

Most people think investing is about picking the right company. That's only half the story. The first, most crucial step is knowing why you are investing. Without a specific purpose, your money is just lazy cash waiting for a snack run. When you give your dollars a mission, they start working like tiny, focused employees.

This is your Investor's Wish List, and it will be the compass that dictates exactly how risky (or safe) your investments need to be.

The core mechanism is simple: the shorter the time until you need the money, the safer that money needs to be. The longer the time horizon, the more risk (and potential reward) you can take.

Let's break down your goals into three essential buckets.

THE 1- TO 3-YEAR GOAL: THE "MUST-HAVE-IT-SOON" CASH

These are your immediate desires—the things you want to buy while you're still living under someone else's roof.

Examples:

1. A state-of-the-art 4K gaming monitor or new console.
2. A specific car fund (saving up for the down payment or first year of insurance).
3. Summer music festival tickets or a specific international trip.

THE STRATEGY: SAFETY FIRST

If you need money within the next three years, the stock market is too volatile. Imagine putting $1,500 toward that new gaming rig, only for the market to dip 20% right before you planned to buy it. Investing for a short-term goal like this is gambling. You cannot risk losing the principal amount.

RISK LEVEL: ULTRA-LOW

For these goals, you are focused on capital preservation and liquidity. This money should live in a high-yield savings account or a Certificate of Deposit (CD). The growth will be slow, but it's guaranteed. It's boring, but it gets the job done without risking your immediate wish list.

THE 3- TO 7-YEAR GOAL: THE MID-RANGE TARGET

This category includes larger, foundational life expenses that are still visible on the horizon.

Examples:

1. Funding the first two years of college tuition or housing.
2. Buying your first reliable used car outright.
3. Starting capital for a small business venture post-graduation.

THE STRATEGY: BALANCED GROWTH

Since you have a few years for the money to recover from any sudden market dips, you can afford to start introducing investment risk. The volatility of the stock market tends to smooth out over a three- to seven-year window, making this the perfect territory for your first investments.

RISK LEVEL: MODERATE

For this money, you might use a 60/40 allocation. This means 60% of the money is focused on growth (invested in broad, diversified funds like the S&P 500), and 40% is kept in safer, stable assets (like bonds or cash equivalents). If the market stumbles, the stable assets provide a cushion. If the market soars, the growth assets capture the upside. This is the compromise zone.

THE 7+ YEAR GOAL: THE FREEDOM MACHINE (YOUR TRUE INVESTING HORIZON)

This is the big game. These are the goals tied to future financial freedom, decades away. This is the money that you should treat as untouchable until you are well into adulthood. This is where the magic of compounding works hardest.

Examples:

1. Retirement (Yes, start thinking about it now—you'll be a millionaire before your friends start reading this chapter).
2. Down payment for a future house or "mansion."
3. Funding a gap year travel experience after college.
4. Future passive income streams.

THE STRATEGY: MAXIMUM GROWTH

When you are 16, you have 40 or 50 years until retirement. A market crash that happens today will be a tiny, irrelevant blip on your financial chart thirty years from now. Because you have time on your side, you can embrace the riskier, but ultimately more rewarding, high-growth assets.

RISK LEVEL: AGGRESSIVE

The primary goal here is to maximize growth. This money should be almost entirely invested in stocks and equity-based funds (upwards of 80% to 100%). You should not panic when the market drops, because when stocks go on sale, you are buying more shares for the long haul.

Your age is your ultimate cheat code. A 50-year-old nearing retirement cannot afford aggressive risk; they need safety. You, however, can absorb market hits and benefit tremendously when the market inevitably bounces back.

The Goal-Setting Mechanism in Action

By setting these goals, you create dedicated buckets for your money. You are no longer just putting money in an account; you are allocating resources toward specific missions.

If you earn $100 this week from a side gig, you don't just dump it all into one place. You decide:

1. $20 goes into the Short-Term bucket (for that new headset)—High-yield savings.
2. $30 goes into the Medium-Term bucket (first car fund)—Moderate index fund investing.
3. $50 goes into the Long-Term bucket (future freedom)—Aggressive stock/ETF investing.

By understanding the relationship between the timeline of the goal and the inherent risk level, you ensure you never have to sell a growth asset at a low price just to pay for an immediate expense. Your wish list isn't just a list of things you want; it is the map for your investment strategy.

CHAPTER TWO

RESOURCE MANAGEMENT MASTERY: YOUR CASH FLOW FUNNEL EXPLAINED (WHY TRACKING $10 NOW SAVES YOU $10,000 LATER)

IF CHAPTER 1 WAS ABOUT GETTING YOUR HEAD RIGHT, CHAPTER 2 IS about making sure your wallet is ready to play ball.

Most people—adults included—treat money like it's a surprise when the bank account hits zero. They have a general idea of how much they make, and an even fuzzier idea of where it all goes. This passive approach is the number one reason people fail to invest. Why? Because you can't deploy resources you don't know you have.

Think of your personal finance as strategic resource management, exactly like in your favorite video game. You wouldn't start a huge quest without checking your inventory, optimizing your gear, and making sure your mana bar is full. Your cash flow funnel is your resource gauge. If you manage $10 efficiently today, identifying where that small ten-dollar bill goes, you are building the skill set that will automatically manage $10,000 efficiently tomorrow.

Before we even look at a stock ticker, we need to locate your "Investment Surplus Number." Let's make tracking your money feel less like homework and more like uncovering hidden loot.

THE HIDDEN LEAK: IDENTIFYING WHICH DOLLARS ARE SABOTAGING YOUR INVESTMENT ACCOUNT (AND HOW TO PLUG THE HOLE)

In the world of wealth, there are two types of people: those who manage their resources and those who let their resources manage them.

If you're waiting until the end of the month to see if you have any money left over to invest, you're already losing. That leftover money is usually zero, because human nature is designed to expand spending to fit the available space. We're going to reverse that. We are going to intentionally create an investment budget first.

To do that, we need to diagnose where your cash is flowing—and where it's leaking.

STEP 1: DETERMINE YOUR INCOME STREAMS (THE RESOURCE INPUT)

As a teen, your income likely falls into one of two categories:

1. Passive Cash (The Stipend): This includes allowance, cash gifts for birthdays, and non-taxable income you receive without clocking in. This income is highly flexible, meaning a larger percentage of it can often go straight to investments.

2. Earned Income (The Grind): This is money from a job, whether it's flipping burgers, babysitting, tutoring, or building websites. This income is often subject to taxes (we'll touch on that later) and is the engine of your future wealth.

Write down every dollar that enters your possession over the course of one month. This is your Gross Income.

STEP 2: TRACK THE EXPENDITURES (THE RESOURCE DRAIN)

THIS IS THE UNCOMFORTABLE BUT NECESSARY PART. FOR THIRTY days—just thirty days—you need to track every single dollar that leaves your hands. If you spend $4.50 on a coffee, track it. If you spend $80 on V-bucks, track it.

Tracking doesn't mean judging. It means diagnosing. You aren't doing this to feel bad about the fun stuff you bought; you are doing it to understand your baseline spending habits.

The easiest way to track this is usually via a banking app that categorizes your spending automatically, or simply by taking a quick photo of every receipt and logging it into a notes app or spreadsheet every evening. If you use cash frequently, you must write it down manually.

After the 30-day tracking period, look at the categories:

Category A: Fixed/Non-Negotiable Costs. (Maybe a monthly phone bill, bus pass, or contribution toward family internet.)

Category B: Discretionary/Wants. (Food delivery, fast-food runs, clothing, entertainment subscriptions, games.)

Category C: Savings/Investing. (Hopefully zero right now, but we are about to change that.)

STEP 3: PLUGGING THE HIDDEN LEAK AND FINDING YOUR SURPLUS

MOST PEOPLE FIND THAT 20% TO 40% OF THEIR SPENDING FALLS into Category B (Wants) and often involves small, repeated purchases that add up—the "Hidden Leak."

Maybe you spend $7 a day, five days a week, on a specialty coffee drink. That's $35 a week, or $140 a month. That $140 isn't just $140. If you invested that $140 monthly from age 16 to age 65, earning a standard 8% average return, that coffee habit cost your future self roughly $800,000!

By identifying and reducing just one small, hidden leak, you have now found your Investment Surplus Number. This is the minimum amount you are guaranteed to have available every month to fund your portfolio.

—★-★-★—

THE 5-MINUTE BUDGET HACK™: HOW TO CONTROL YOUR SPENDING WITHOUT FEELING POOR

WHEN MOST PEOPLE HEAR THE WORD "BUDGET," THEY PICTURE A REstrictive, joy-killing chore. They imagine eating dry toast and canceling their Netflix subscription. We are going to change that narrative.

Budgeting is not deprivation; it is permission. It's permission to spend money on things that matter, because you already took care of the things that matter most—your future.

Our goal is to implement a high-impact, low-friction system. We call this the 5-Minute Budget Hack™ because it should take minimal time and zero effort once set up.

THE TEEN 50/30/20 RULE REMIX

YOU MAY HAVE HEARD OF THE CLASSIC 50/30/20 RULE. WE'RE ADAPTing it because your financial life right now is simpler than that of an adult paying rent and mortgages.

The goal is to sort your Gross Income immediately upon receiving it:

1. 20% to Future Self (Investment & Long-Term Savings): This is the most important bucket. This money is untouchable and goes directly into your long-term portfolio.

2. 30% to Short-Term Goals (Savings for Wants): This is the fund for your next big purchase: concert tickets, a new gaming console, or a spring break trip. This money stays in an easily accessible savings account, and is what prevents you from dipping into your 20% investment bucket.

3. 50% to Living/Discretionary: This covers all your necessary immediate spending and the guilt-free "fun money" for the month. This includes gas, minor family contributions, and daily fast-food runs.

Why does this work? Because you pre-invest the money before you even see it. Whatever is left in the 50% bucket is yours to spend without remorse. If you blow it all on pizza in the first week, that's fine! Your investments are still secure, and you just have to manage without any extra spending for the next three weeks. This is the definition of control.

IMPLEMENTING THE HACK WITH TECHNOLOGY

SINCE YOU ARE DIGITALLY NATIVE, MANUAL LEDGER BOOKS ARE A waste of time. Utilize these modern tools:

Banking App Categorization: Most modern bank accounts automatically categorize your spending (groceries, entertainment, bills). Use these built-in features to monitor your 50% category spending quickly.

Note-Taking Automation: Use a simple Notes app on your phone. Every day, make a quick entry of your spending. You don't need fancy software; consistency beats complexity.

Envelope/Jar System (Digital Edition): Set up separate bank accounts or savings folders (if your bank allows) labeled "Investment," "Gaming PC Fund," and "Spending." When your income hits, manually or automatically transfer the 20% and 30% first. This creates a visual separation, ensuring that money is psychologically untouchable.

—★-★-★—

WARNING: THE 'INTEREST VIRUS' THAT INSTANTLY KILLS COMPOUNDING (AND HOW TO IMMUNIZE YOUR FINANCES)

In Chapter 1, we celebrated the magic of compounding interest—that wonderful engine that makes money grow exponentially while you sleep.

Debt is the mirror image of compounding interest. Debt is reverse compounding. It is the "Interest Virus" that works tirelessly against you, ensuring that you pay more for everything and that your money shrinks while you sleep.

To succeed in investing, you must adopt one foundational rule: Avoid high-interest debt like it is literal poison.

GOOD DEBT VS. BAD DEBT

Not all debt is automatically evil, though as a teenager, your exposure should be minimal.

Good Debt (The Accelerator): This is debt used to acquire assets that appreciate or increase your long-term earning power (e.g., student loans for a high-value degree, a reasonable mortgage to buy a home).

Bad Debt (The Destroyer): This is debt used to purchase consumable liabilities—things that immediately lose value (e.g., high-interest credit card debt, payday loans, buying a depreciating asset like a car on expensive finance).

The most immediate danger to a young investor is high-interest consumer debt. While traditional credit card debt might be less common for minors, the principle applies to any high-cost borrowing. This might manifest as:

1. "Buy Now, Pay Later" Apps: These often entice users with zero interest, but if you miss a payment, the fees and interest rates can skyrocket and become predatory.

2. Late Fees and Overdrafts: Banks charge enormous penalties for small mistakes. These $35 fees are essentially high-interest loans that steal directly from your potential investment fund.

3. Borrowing from Friends/Family at Punitive Rates: If you borrow $100 and have to pay back $120 next week, that is a 20% interest rate in seven days!

WHY DEBT KILLS YOUR INVESTMENT POTENTIAL

If your investment earns 8% annually, but you are carrying consumer debt that costs 18% annually, you are losing money overall. You must pay that 18% debt before you can realize the 8% gain.

IMMUNIZATION PROTOCOL: PRIORITIZE DEBT ZERO

If you currently have any high-interest debt (not including a responsible car payment or student loan), your first priority is not investing. Your first priority is clearing that debt.

Think of it this way: Paying off debt with an 18% interest rate is the equivalent of making an investment that guarantees an 18% tax-free return —something you will never find in the stock market. Get rid of the virus before you start building. Once the debt is zeroed out, your money is now immunized and ready to deploy for growth.

—★-★-★—

THE 'PAY YOURSELF FIRST' MANDATE: THE SINGLE RULE THAT FORCES YOU TO GET RICH

We've found the hidden money (the surplus), we've budgeted it (the 50/30/20 rule), and we've immunized it against the Interest Virus (avoiding debt). Now, we execute the final foundational rule: The Pay Yourself First Mandate.

This is the principle that transforms average savers into consistent investors.

Most people operate using this equation:

Income - Expenses = Leftovers (Savings/Investment)

As we learned, "Leftovers" usually equals zero. The correct equation for guaranteed wealth creation must be flipped:

Income - Investment = Spending (Leftovers)

This means when money hits your account, the 20% designated for investment moves immediately to the investment bucket, regardless of upcoming expenses. Only the remaining 80% is available for your lifestyle.

DEFINING THE BUCKETS: SAVINGS VS. INVESTMENT

While both savings and investing involve putting money aside, they serve fundamentally different purposes based on their timeline and safety level.

The Savings Bucket (The Emergency Reserve)

Purpose: Safety, liquidity, and short-term goals (under 5 years).

Goal: Hold liquid cash for true emergencies (a broken phone, car trouble, unexpected bills) or short-term purchases (the gaming PC).

Location: A high-yield savings account (HYSA). The growth rate is low (maybe 4-5%), but the risk is zero. This money is protected from market downturns.

Mandate: You should try to build an emergency fund equal to one to three months of your necessary expenses. Since teens typically have lower fixed expenses, even $500 to $1,000 can serve as a robust shield.

THE INVESTMENT BUCKET (THE WEALTH ENGINE)

PURPOSE: GROWTH, COMPOUNDING, AND LONG-TERM FINANCIAL freedom (over 5 years).

Goal: Accumulate assets that generate returns (stocks, funds).

Location: Your brokerage account (Chapter 3).

Mandate: This money is allocated to higher-risk, higher-return assets and is expected to stay there for decades.

Why is this crucial? If you don't have a savings safety net, the moment life throws you a curveball, you will be forced to sell your investments at the wrong time (likely when the market is down) to cover the expense. The savings bucket acts as the iron shield protecting your portfolio.

By implementing the Pay Yourself First Mandate, you are essentially making an unbreakable contract with your future self. You are leveraging systems—not willpower—to guarantee that money is working for you, every time you get paid. You have now optimized your resource management funnel and are ready to move on to the practical step: opening the account where your newly found capital will begin compounding.

THE HIDDEN LEAK: IDENTIFYING WHICH DOLLARS ARE SABOTAGING YOUR INVESTMENT ACCOUNT (AND HOW TO PLUG THE HOLE)

If you're ready to become an investor, the very first step isn't opening a brokerage account—it's performing a forensic audit on your own wallet.

Think of your cash flow like a sophisticated plumbing system. If you want to fill the investment tank, you first have to make sure the water pressure is good and that there aren't any sneaky, hidden leaks letting dollars drip onto the sidewalk.

For most young people, money enters the system through two very distinct pipes. Understanding which pipe your money comes from is essential, because we tend to treat them differently.

The first pipe is your Earned Income. This is the stuff you trade your actual time and sweat for. If you have a part-time job flipping burgers, tutoring geometry, coding websites, or walking dogs, that money is earned. You feel the weight of it because you worked for it. You are generally more careful with it, precisely because you remember waking up early on a Saturday to get it.

The second pipe is Passive Cash. This includes your weekly or monthly allowance, birthday checks from Grandma, or the $50 your dad gave you for cleaning the garage. This money often feels like "free money." It arrives in your hands without the direct, recent effort of a time trade-off.

And here is where the sabotage begins.

The hidden leak in 90% of teen finances is the Passive Cash.

Because it feels like a windfall, it is the easiest money to waste on impulsive, low-value purchases. That extra $20 allowance? It disappears on three lattes and an in-app purchase you won't remember by next week. The $100 birthday check? It evaporates into a vague shopping trip that leaves you with nothing tangible, and certainly nothing invested.

When you don't track passive cash, you mentally assign it zero value. It never makes it to the savings account, and it certainly never makes it to the investment account. This is the dollar leakage that can cost you tens of thousands in future wealth. That $100, if invested today and compounding for the next 40 years, is worth far more than that random haul from the mall.

Plugging the Hole: Calculating Your Investable Resources

To stop the leak, you must treat every single dollar—earned or passive—with the same respect and attention. This requires combining both streams and then calculating your true disposable income for investing.

STEP 1: TALLY YOUR TOTAL INCOME

Add up everything you receive in a month:

Wages from your job (Earned)

Allowance (Passive)

Regular side-gig income (Earned)

Any other cash gifts or regular income streams (Passive)

STEP 2: IDENTIFY NON-NEGOTIABLE EXPENSES

Since you are likely living under your parents' roof, your necessary expenses are far lower than an adult's, which is your massive advantage! These necessary expenses are the dollars that absolutely must leave your account for survival or basic commitments.

Phone bill (if you pay it)

Gas/Commuting costs

Lunch money/Necessary food costs

Debt payments (if applicable, though ideally this is zero, as Chapter 2.3 will discuss)

STEP 3: CALCULATE DISPOSABLE INCOME

TOTAL INCOME - NON-NEGOTIABLE EXPENSES = DISPOSABLE INCOME

This Disposable Income number is the pool of resources you have complete control over. It is the money that currently gets split between investing, short-term savings (like saving for a new gaming console), and lifestyle spending (fun money).

This is the point where most people fail. They wait until the end of the month to see what's left over to invest. But if you wait until the end, there is never anything left over, because the hidden leak (impulse consumer spending) has already drained the tank.

The professional investor, however, operates under the "Pay Yourself First" mandate (which we cover in detail later). The key strategy here is to immediately ring-fence a portion of that Disposable Income for investment.

Let's say your Disposable Income is $400 this month. Before you even think about buying a new pair of shoes or upgrading your gear, you should assign $100 to the "Investment Bucket." This $100 is now off-limits. It is a commitment. It is the dollar that goes toward buying an ownership stake in Apple, not just another pair of AirPods.

By recognizing that passive cash and earned income are equally valuable and by calculating the total amount you have control over, you transform from a passive consumer into an active resource manager. You are not just tracking your money; you are strategically deploying your assets to sabotage your future self's poverty. The leak is plugged. Now let's figure out how to manage the flow.

—★-★-★—

THE 5-MINUTE BUDGET HACK™: HOW TO CONTROL YOUR SPENDING WITHOUT FEELING POOR

IF YOU HEAR THE WORD "BUDGETING" AND INSTANTLY PICTURE YOUR grandparents balancing a check book while looking mournful, you are not alone. Most people treat budgeting like a financial prison—a set of rules designed solely to prevent joy.

But let's flip the script. Budgeting is not about deprivation; it's about control. It's the difference between driving a car with a clear navigation screen versus driving blindfolded. When you know exactly where your resources are, you gain the power to direct them towards what you truly want—whether that's a new gaming PC next month or a massive investment portfolio 15 years from now.

The traditional, painful way of budgeting is dead. We are going to use two modern, low-effort strategies to automate your cash flow funnel.

The goal? Spend five minutes setting up the system, then let the system do the heavy lifting.

1. THE MODERN TRACKER: APPS THAT DO THE MATH FOR YOU

FORGET NOTEBOOKS AND SPREADSHEETS. YOU NEED A SYSTEM THAT tracks your money passively. Since most teens are dealing with allowances, part-time job income deposited directly, or digital payment methods like Venmo/Cash App, the data is already digital.

The Power of Awareness: You don't need to drastically change your spending habits on Day 1. You just need to know them. Tracking is simply taking inventory. When you see in black and white that you spent $60 on delivery food last week, it hits differently than just shrugging it off.

Your Actionable 2-Minute Plan:

1. Check Your Bank/App Stats: Many modern banking apps (and specialized tracking apps like Mint or YNAB, if your custodial parent allows) can automatically categorize your spending. Look at the graphs they generate. What's your biggest expense category outside of essentials?

2. The Screenshot Audit: If you don't use a banking app, take three minutes once a week to scroll through your transaction history in whatever method you use (debit card, Apple Pay, etc.). Create three simple labels:

Essential: Bills, gas, necessary school items.

Fun: Everything else (Starbucks, movies, games).

Investable: What's left over.

This simple triage exercise instantly shows you where the fat is—the non-essential dollars that could be working for you instead.

2. THE 50/30/20 RULE: THE TEEN INVESTMENT MANDATE

Once you know where your money goes, it's time to give every new dollar a mission. This hack is based on the tried-and-true 50/30/20 principle, modified specifically for a teen's financial structure where rent and mortgages aren't usually a factor.

Your income—whether it's earned, gifted, or allowance—is 100%. Here is how you strategically divide it:

A. 50% ESSENTIALS & SHORT-TERM GOALS (THE SAFETY NET)

SINCE YOU LIKELY DON'T HAVE UTILITY BILLS, THIS CATEGORY covers your direct financial responsibilities and immediate, short-term wants (things you plan to buy in the next few months).

Fixed Essentials: Phone bill contribution, bus passes, gas for your car, gym membership.

Buffer Money: Money to cover unexpected necessary expenses.

Short-Term Goals: Saving up for that PS5, new snowboard, or concert tickets. This pool keeps you from draining your fun money or, worse, dipping into your investments.

Why 50%? Because having a healthy pool of accessible cash prevents you from feeling restricted. You can still buy the things you want, but you budget for them deliberately.

B. 30% FUN, FREEDOM, AND GUILT-FREE SPENDING (THE JOY ZONE)

THIS IS THE MOST IMPORTANT CATEGORY FOR PSYCHOLOGICAL health. This 30% is your allowance for impulse buys, entertainment, fast food, and spontaneous outings.

The beauty of the 50/30/20 rule is that once you set aside your Essentials and your Future Fund (see next point), you can spend this 30% however you want, completely guilt-free.

This eliminates the mental drag of constantly questioning every small purchase. If you budget $100 for fun this week and you spend it all on pizza and a movie, that's fine! You've already paid your future self, which leads us to the most crucial part...

C. 20% THE PAY YOURSELF FIRST MANDATE (THE INVESTMENT ENGINE)

THIS IS THE NON-NEGOTIABLE MINIMUM. EVERY DOLLAR YOU EARN, the first 20 cents of it must go into your future fund.

This 20% should be split between two buckets:

1. Investment Bucket: The majority of this 20% goes directly into your brokerage account, ready to be deployed into stocks and funds (as we will detail in Chapters 6 and 7). This is your wealth engine.

2. Emergency Savings: A smaller portion (maybe 5% of your total income) should build up a small, liquid emergency fund—money you can access immediately if your laptop dies or your car breaks down. This protects your investment account from being liquidated when minor crises arise.

THE STRATEGIC SHIFT: FROM CONSUMER TO COMMANDER

THE 5-MINUTE BUDGET HACK™ TRANSFORMS YOUR SPENDING FROM reactive to proactive. When you earn $100, instead of letting it sit randomly in your bank account until it vanishes, you immediately assign:

$50 to immediate needs/goals.

$30 to guilt-free spending.

$20 straight into the investment account.

By setting this up right away, you eliminate the temptation to spend your investing money. You are leveraging a fundamental psychological truth: You cannot spend money that you never see.

This system doesn't make you feel poor; it makes you feel powerful. You are no longer reacting to your bank balance; you are strategically commanding your resources, ensuring that your present self enjoys life while your future self gets rich.

—★-★-★—

WARNING: THE 'INTEREST VIRUS' THAT INSTANTLY KILLS COMPOUNDING (AND HOW TO IMMUNIZE YOUR FINANCES)

IMAGINE COMPOUNDING INTEREST IS YOUR FINANCIAL SUPERHERO, A powerful engine that accelerates your money over time. Now imagine a microscopic organism that enters your system and begins to immediately reverse that engine, grinding your progress to a halt and demanding payment just to stop the bleeding.

That is high-interest debt, or what we call the "Interest Virus."

The core mechanism of wealth building for a young investor is compounding. We know this engine usually runs at a reliable pace, perhaps generating 7% to 10% annual returns. The Interest Virus is lethal because its symptoms—the interest rates charged on consumption debt—often run between 15% and 30%.

Mathematically, if you are paying 20% interest on a debt, you must earn more than 20% on your investments just to break even. This is not investing; it is financial damage control, and it instantly kills the power of compounding. If you invest $100 and earn $7 in a year, but you simultaneously pay $20 in interest on a loan, you aren't compounding. You are losing money. You are in a state of negative compounding.

The single, non-negotiable immunization required before you even consider buying your first share is simple: become debt-free, especially of high-interest consumer debt.

The key to preventing this infection is understanding the difference between good debt and bad debt.

THE GOOD DEBT (THE IMMUNITY BOOSTER)

Good debt is debt used to acquire an asset that generates income or increases in value over time. It is essentially an investment in future wealth.

Examples (often relevant later in life):

1. Mortgages: Borrowing money to buy real estate that usually appreciates in value and can generate rental income.

2. Education Loans: Borrowing money (at reasonable rates) to get a degree or vocational training that dramatically increases your lifetime earning potential.

3. Business Loans: Borrowing capital to launch or expand a legitimate business that will generate profits.

Good debt is typically characterized by a low interest rate and the fact that the purchased item is a value-increasing asset.

THE BAD DEBT (THE VIRUS)

Bad debt is money borrowed to purchase consumables—things that quickly lose value (depreciate) or are used up. This debt is the killer because it often comes with punishingly high interest rates and leaves you with nothing of value once the item is gone.

For teens, the primary source of bad debt might not be a traditional credit card (yet), but the principle is the same and takes many forms:

1. High-Interest Store Financing: Financing a new $1,200 gaming laptop over 12 months, only to find the interest and fees bump the final price to $1,500. The laptop is already outdated by the time you pay it off.

2. Buy-Now-Pay-Later (BNPL) Services: These popular services, often advertised as interest-free, can charge massive late fees or ballooning interest

if payment schedules are missed. You bought that cool jacket, and now it costs 40% more because you missed a deadline.

3. Personal Loans/High-Interest Borrowing: Even borrowing $50 from a friend or a family member who tacks on a large, informal interest fee because they know you're desperate. Never underestimate how quickly small, high-interest obligations can derail your plans.

The rule is simple: If you borrow money to buy something that you will consume or that will lose value rapidly, you are contracting the Interest Virus.

THE IMMUNIZATION PLAN: ZERO DEBT, MAXIMUM COMPOUNDING

Your investment journey begins with a clean slate. You cannot win the wealth game while paying the bank or a lender more interest than your investments are generating.

The "Pay Yourself First" rule we will discuss in the next section is conditional: The very first person you must pay is whoever holds your debt.

Therefore, follow this debt-elimination hierarchy:

STEP 1: THE EMERGENCY DISINFECTANT

Stop all non-essential purchases immediately. Calculate exactly how much you owe and to whom. If the interest rate is above 10% (the average return of the stock market), that debt is your immediate, number-one financial enemy.

STEP 2: THE SNOWBALL OR AVALANCHE STRATEGY (THE CURE)

There are two popular ways to kill debt. The "Snowball" method involves paying off the smallest debt first to gain emotional momentum. The "Avalanche" method involves attacking the debt with the highest interest rate first, which saves the most money mathematically. As a serious investor, you should choose the Avalanche method to neutralize the most potent part of the Virus immediately. Redirect all available disposable income toward that highest-interest debt.

STEP 3: THE INVESTMENT STANDOFF

Until all high-interest consumer debt is annihilated, your investment account remains mostly empty. Every single spare dollar you have must go toward paying down that debt. Once you are fully immunized—meaning your personal balance sheet is clean—then, and only then, can your compounding engine run freely and powerfully.

Remember: Compounding is magic when it works for you. It is devastating when it works against you, fuelled by the Interest Virus. Avoid bad debt, and your journey to wealth becomes immeasurably easier.

THE 'PAY YOURSELF FIRST' MANDATE: THE SINGLE RULE THAT FORCES YOU TO GET RICH

You've done the hard work of tracking your cash flow and identifying where your money comes from and where it currently disappears. Now, we must install the operating system upgrade that turns a sporadic habit into an automatic wealth machine. This is the single most important habit you will ever develop, and it is called the "Pay Yourself First" mandate.

To understand why this is mandatory, we first need to define two separate roles for your money. Think of your finances as two completely different buckets, each serving a vital purpose.

THE SAFETY STASH: YOUR SAVINGS BUCKET

This bucket is for the boring stuff, the immediate needs, and the financial crash helmet. This money needs to be entirely safe and easily accessible.

Role: Emergency funds, short-term goals (anything you need in the next 1 to 3 years).

Goals: Buying that high-end gaming console next year, saving up for a car, funding college application fees, or having cash ready for unexpected expenses (like replacing a broken laptop).

Location: High-yield savings accounts or money market funds. Safe, liquid, and boring—exactly what you want.

Purpose: To prevent you from having to sell your investments at a loss when life throws a curveball.

THE GROWTH ENGINE: YOUR INVESTMENT BUCKET

This is where the magic happens. This bucket is for financial freedom, long-term wealth creation, and letting compounding interest do its job over decades.

Role: Long-term wealth generation (anything you won't need for 5+ years).

Goals: Funding retirement, down payment on a house in your twenties, or reaching financial independence.

Location: Your brokerage or custodial investment account (Chapter 3).

Purpose: To generate returns that outpace inflation and turn your spare cash into a fortune.

The cardinal sin most people commit is confusing these two buckets. They put their rent money in the stock market (too risky!) or they leave their long-term wealth in a savings account (too low growth!). Keep them separate, keep their purposes distinct.

THE MANDATE: PAYING FUTURE YOU

THE "PAY YOURSELF FIRST" RULE IS SIMPLE YET REVOLUTIONARY. It dictates that the very first people you pay when you receive income are you and future you.

Most people follow the standard consumption pattern:

1. Get Paid (Allowance, Paycheck).
2. Pay Bills/Expenses (Phone, Gas, Food, Streaming).
3. Buy Stuff (New shoes, games, snacks).
4. If there is anything left over, maybe save or invest it.

As you learned in Chapter 2, waiting until step four ensures the money is never there. Every dollar you see is a dollar tempting you to spend it.

The "Pay Yourself First" system flips this script:

1. Get Paid (Allowance, Paycheck).
2. Pay Future You (Investment/Savings Transfer—this is your mandatory "bill").
3. Pay Bills/Expenses.
4. Buy Stuff with the remaining funds.

By treating your savings and investments as non-negotiable expenses—just like your phone bill or gas money—you force yourself into a pattern of wealth creation. The amount you allocate to consumption is reduced, but the financial benefit to your future self is maximized.

—★-★-★—

HOW TO FORCE YOURSELF TO GET RICH

THIS RULE ONLY WORKS IF IT IS MANDATORY, WHICH MEANS IT MUST be automated. You must remove the decision-making process entirely.

Let's say you currently earn $400 per month from a part-time job or allowance.

The Pay Yourself First system looks like this:

Step 1: Determine Your Investment Percentage. A good starting point for teens with low expenses is to dedicate 20% to 30% of their earned income toward the two buckets. Let's aim for 25%.

Step 2: Allocate Between the Buckets. You need some liquid savings, but since you are young and your goals are long-term, the Growth Engine should receive the lion's share.

Savings (Safety Stash): 5% of income ($20)

Investment (Growth Engine): 20% of income ($80)

Step 3: Automate the Transfer. The moment that $400 hits your bank account, you must have automatic transfers set up:

$20 automatically transfers to your high-yield savings account.

$80 automatically transfers directly into your custodial brokerage account.

The remaining $300 is what you use for everything else (spending, fun, bills). You literally never see the money dedicated to investment. It goes straight from the source to the investment bucket, where it is instantly put to work via compounding interest.

This simple, automated rule solves 90% of the problems people have with managing money. It ensures consistency, eliminates procrastination, and guarantees that even if you spend the rest of your cash on impulse buys, you are still building the foundation of a future fortune. If you stick to this mandate, the math of compounding will guarantee your success. You will be rich because you made it the first, non-negotiable priority.

CHAPTER THREE

THE VAULT KEY: SETTING UP YOUR SECURE, LEGAL INVESTMENT ACCOUNT (BYPASSING THE ADULT PAPERWORK NIGHTMARE)

THE INTRODUCTION OF THIS BOOK WAS ABOUT UNLOCKING YOUR FInancial superpower. Chapter 1 was about the math, and Chapter 2 was about finding the cash. Now, we've reached the gatekeeper. To actually deploy your money into the stock market, you need a safe, legal place to hold those assets. You need a brokerage account.

Think of a brokerage like a specialized bank for stocks and funds. Regular banks handle deposits and loans; brokerages handle buying and selling financial assets. Since you are under 18, you can't just walk up and open an account on your own—the government still insists on parental oversight for large financial decisions.

This chapter is your Vault Key. We are going to demystify the required adult involvement and provide the specific names and platforms that make this process as painless as possible. Setting up the account is often the single biggest hurdle young investors face. Once this is done, the path to wealth is wide open.

—★-★-★—

DISCOVERED: THE TOP 3 TEEN-FRIENDLY BROKERAGE PLATFORMS WITH ZERO FEES

In the dark ages of investing (like 10 years ago), brokerages charged fees just to make a trade. If you only had $50 to invest, paying a $7 commission was a painful 14% loss before you even started.

Today, thanks to the explosion of online platforms, most major brokerages offer zero-commission trading on stocks and ETFs (Exchange-Traded Funds). This is fantastic news for teen investors starting with small amounts.

However, not all brokerages are equal when it comes to custodial accounts—the type you need. We are looking for platforms that are secure, easy to use, have low or zero minimum deposits, and offer educational tools to help you learn as you go.

Here are the gold standard choices for setting up a secure investment vault:

1. FIDELITY INVESTMENTS

Why it's great for teens: Fidelity is one of the largest and most respected financial institutions globally. They offer excellent, commission-free brokerage accounts (often called Youth Accounts) that are structured as a standard UGMA/UTMA account (we'll explain that acronym shortly). Crucially, Fidelity has robust educational content and, more recently, launched specific products designed for teens that allow for a high degree of independent management under the custodian's watchful eye. They are professional, secure, and offer an incredible range of investment choices.

2. CHARLES SCHWAB

Why it's great for teens: Like Fidelity, Schwab is a titan in the industry, offering a full suite of custodial accounts. They excel in customer service and provide exceptional research tools—a feature you'll use later when you start researching individual stocks. Schwab is known for its investor-friendly approach, making them a safe and reliable choice for beginners. Their platform is clean and intuitive, reducing the confusion that often comes with complex financial interfaces.

3. VANGUARD

Why it's great for teens: Vanguard is the low-cost champion, founded on the principle of minimizing fees for investors. While their user interface might feel slightly less flashy than some newer apps, their commitment to low-cost index funds is unparalleled. If your strategy is primarily focused on the "Lazy Genius Strategy" (investing in broad market funds, as we discuss in Chapter 4), Vanguard is the ultimate platform for maximizing your returns by keeping costs near zero. They are reliable, stable, and focused on long-term wealth accumulation.

A Note on Apps and Specialized Platforms:

You may see newer investing apps advertised (like Robinhood or Public). While these often have flashy interfaces, many do not easily support the custodial account structure required for minors, or their educational resources are limited. For your first official investment account, prioritize the established brokerages that are experts in legal compliance and long-term security. These platforms are built for decades of growth, not just trendy day trading.

The final decision should come down to which platform your parent or guardian (the future Custodian) is most comfortable with, or which one offers the simplest user experience. Since all three listed above are free to open and operate, there is no major monetary difference—only slight differences in interface and research tools.

—★-★-★—

THE 'PARENT TRAP' INVESTMENT ACCOUNT: HOW TO GET YOUR FIRST $1,000 INVESTED LEGALLY (THE UGMA/UTMA PLAYBOOK)

ALRIGHT, LET'S TALK LEGALITIES. AS A MINOR, YOU CANNOT ENTER into a contract for the purpose of trading stocks. Therefore, any money you invest must be held in a custodial account. This is the government's way of ensuring an adult takes legal responsibility for the account until you reach the age of majority (usually 18 or 21, depending on your state).

These accounts are most commonly known as UGMA (Uniform Gifts to Minors Act) or UTMA (Uniform Transfers to Minors Act) accounts. The difference between them is minor, but essentially, the UTMA is slightly more flexible in terms of the assets it can hold (sometimes including real estate or other property, though for stock investing they function identically).

Here is the vital takeaway about the Custodial Account:

The money in the account legally belongs to you the moment it is deposited.

This is the key point that separates a custodial account from a parent's joint bank account. When your parents open a UGMA/UTMA in your name, they are legally making an irrevocable gift. They cannot later decide to take the money back for their own use, or for the college fund of your younger sibling. The account is titled: "[Custodian Name], Custodian FBO (For Benefit Of) [Your Name]."

ROLES AND RESPONSIBILITIES DEMYSTIFIED

1. The Minor (You) — The Beneficial Owner

Your role is to decide what to invest in. You are the future recipient of the wealth. You are the strategist, the researcher, and the ultimate beneficiary. While the custodian signs the paperwork, you should be doing the heavy lifting in terms of investment education and stock selection (using the guidance in this book).

2. The Custodian (The Adult) — The Account Manager

The custodian (usually a parent or legal guardian) has two main responsibilities:

A. The Paperwork: They sign the legal documents to open the account and are responsible for managing any administrative tasks, like confirming trades or handling tax forms (though the tax liability often falls to you, the minor, once income thresholds are met—more on that in Chapter 8).

B. Fiduciary Duty: They must manage the assets solely in the best interest of the minor (you). This means they can't make reckless, high-risk trades that aren't suitable for a young person's long-term plan. They hold the legal control until you "age out" of the account.

THE AGE-OUT CLAUSE: THE FINISH LINE

The moment you hit the age of majority (usually 18, but sometimes 21 or 25 depending on the state and the specific account terms), the custodian's control vanishes. The account automatically transfers directly into your name, and you assume full, independent legal control over every asset. This transfer is one of the most exciting financial milestones for a young investor.

Getting past the paperwork is simply a matter of sitting down with your chosen custodian and the brokerage's online application. It requires their personal details (address, Social Security Number, photo ID) and your details (Social Security Number). It may feel like an adult chore, but it is a necessary, one-time step that unlocks decades of compounding growth.

—★-★-★—

THE ANTI-SCAMMER CHECKLIST: 7 CRITICAL SECURITY STEPS TO PROTECT YOUR PORTFOLIO FROM DIGITAL THIEVES

You are a digital native, which means you are probably already hyper-aware of digital security. But when money is involved, the stakes are higher. Cybercriminals and scammers love investors, especially new ones, because they often use emotion and FOMO (Fear of Missing Out) to trick people into giving up their funds.

Protecting your investment portfolio is non-negotiable. Here is your essential seven-point security checklist:

1. MANDATORY TWO-FACTOR AUTHENTICATION (2FA)

This is the single most important security measure. 2FA means that even if a thief steals your password, they still cannot access your account without a second code sent to your physical phone or a dedicated security app. Set this up immediately upon opening your brokerage account. Never use SMS text messages for 2FA; use an authenticator app (like Google Authenticator or Authy) if the brokerage supports it.

2. UNIQUE, COMPLEX PASSWORDS

Do not reuse your Instagram or gaming password for your investment account. Your brokerage password should be long, complex, and unique. Use a password manager (like 1Password or LastPass) to generate and store it securely.

3. RECOGNIZE PHISHING SCAMS

Phishing is when someone pretends to be a reputable source (like your brokerage) to steal your information. Always assume an email or text message asking for account details is fake. Brokerages will never email you requesting your password or account number. If you receive a suspicious message, do not click the link—instead, navigate directly to your brokerage's official website by typing the address yourself.

4. THE 'TOO GOOD TO BE TRUE' RULE

If someone on a forum, Discord server, or via a DM tells you about a "secret stock" or a "guaranteed 1,000% return crypto coin," they are trying to scam you. Real investing is slow and boring, not exciting and high-stakes. Scams often promise immediate, massive returns. Ignore them.

5. SECURE YOUR DEVICES

Make sure the computer or phone you use to access your financial accounts is running the latest operating system updates and has adequate antivirus/anti-malware protection. Updates often include critical security patches.

6. PRIVATE NETWORK ONLY

Never log into your brokerage account when connected to public Wi-Fi (like at a coffee shop or school library). These networks are often unsecured and are hotbeds for digital eavesdropping. Only manage your money on a secure, private, password-protected network.

7. MONITOR ACCOUNT ACTIVITY

Get in the habit of quickly reviewing your brokerage statement monthly. Look for trades or withdrawals that you or your custodian did not authorize. Early detection is key to mitigating any unauthorized activity.

—★-★-★—

THE 14-MINUTE ACCOUNT SETUP: YOUR ZERO-FRICTION CHECKLIST TO FUNDING YOUR VERY FIRST TRADE

You've chosen your brokerage (Fidelity, Schwab, or Vanguard), and you have your custodian ready to go. Now, we execute. The whole process, start to finish, should take less time than watching an episode of your favorite show.

Here is the step-by-step checklist to move from zero to funded account:

STEP 1: GATHER DOCUMENTATION (5 MINUTES)

Before you sit down at the computer, have these pieces of information ready.

For the Minor (You):

Full Legal Name, Address, and Date of Birth

Social Security Number (SSN)

For the Custodian (Adult):

Full Legal Name, Address, and Date of Birth

Social Security Number (SSN)

Driver's License or Government ID details

STEP 2: CHOOSE THE ACCOUNT TYPE (1 MINUTE)

When you navigate to the brokerage's 'Open an Account' section, select the option for a Custodial Account, usually listed under "Accounts for Minors" or "UGMA/UTMA." Do not select a standard individual account (you're too young) or a retirement account (not yet).

STEP 3: COMPLETE THE APPLICATION (5 MINUTES)

Fill in the requested details for both the minor and the custodian. The online forms are straightforward and primarily focus on identity verification. You will need to specify your relationship to the minor (e.g., Parent, Guardian). Most brokerages handle the custodian verification immediately via electronic checks.

STEP 4: LINK YOUR FUNDING SOURCE (2 MINUTES)

This is where the money moves from your checking or savings account into the brokerage vault. You will need the routing number and account number of your bank account. Follow the on-screen prompts to link the accounts securely. The brokerage will often send two small "test deposits" ($0.03, $0.15) to your bank account, which you must verify a day or two later to confirm ownership.

STEP 5: FUND THE ACCOUNT (1 MINUTE)

Decide on your initial deposit. Remember Chapter 2—this should be money you have allocated specifically for long-term investment. Initiate the transfer. Standard ACH transfers can take 1–3 business days to clear, but once the transfer is initiated, most brokerages will allow you to make your first trade immediately using the unsettled funds.

Congratulations. You now have a secure, legal investment vehicle. The toughest administrative hurdle is now behind you. The account is open, the money is on the way, and you are ready to learn what to buy in the next chapter.

—★-★-★—

DISCOVERED: THE TOP 3 TEEN-FRIENDLY BROKERAGE PLATFORMS WITH ZERO FEES

THE GOOD NEWS IS THAT INVESTING HAS NEVER BEEN CHEAPER. THE era of paying $10 or $20 commission fees for every single trade is thankfully over. For the purposes of stock, ETF (Exchange-Traded Fund), and mutual fund investing, the top-tier brokerages are essentially free.

Therefore, the choice of platform shouldn't be based on cost, but on features, ease of use, and, critically, how well they handle custodial accounts (UTMA/UGMA), which is the necessary legal gateway for you to invest before you turn 18.

Here is a breakdown of the three market leaders that are best suited for the young investor.

FIDELITY: THE MODERN GOLD STANDARD

FIDELITY IS OFTEN THE FIRST STOP FOR SAVVY YOUNG INVESTORS, largely due to its commitment to low costs and the best combination of educational resources and accessibility.

Key Features for Teens:

Zero Commissions. Fidelity offers $0 commissions on stock, ETF, and option trades.

Fractional Shares. This is a game-changer. Fidelity allows you to buy stocks "by the slice" (fractional shares). If Apple stock is trading at $170, but you only have $25 to invest, you can buy $25 worth of Apple. This is essential for maximizing small, frequent contributions.

Fidelity Youth Account. For teens aged 13–17, Fidelity offers a specialized account that the teen manages, linked to a custodial account, providing incredible practical experience.

Educational Content. Fidelity's Learning Center is vast and high-quality, covering everything from basic definitions to advanced research.

Ideal for: Teens who want a great mobile app experience, the ability to trade fractional shares, and a wealth of educational tools to guide them through the learning process.

Charles Schwab: The Research Powerhouse

Schwab is one of the most established financial institutions in the world and offers an extremely stable, high-tech platform that rivals Fidelity. While they may not have the dedicated "teen" branding, their core custodial account features are second to none.

Key Features for Teens:

Zero Commissions. Consistent $0 trading commissions for stocks and ETFs.

Excellent Research Tools. Schwab is famous for its in-depth market analysis and research reports. As you move beyond basic index funds, Schwab provides powerful tools (like StreetSmart Edge) for digging into specific companies.

Broad Investment Selection. Schwab offers a huge range of investments, including thousands of low-cost Schwab ETFs and mutual funds.

Strong Customer Service. They have a reputation for top-tier support, which is helpful when your custodian (parent/guardian) has questions about the setup process.

Ideal for: Teens who want to eventually become serious researchers and analysts, or those whose family already utilizes Schwab for other accounts, simplifying the custodial setup.

VANGUARD: THE PASSIVE WEALTH BUILDER'S CHOICE

VANGUARD IS UNIQUE BECAUSE THE COMPANY IS OWNED BY ITS funds, meaning their primary mission is to keep costs low for investors. While their app experience is sometimes less flashy than Schwab or Fidelity, their focus on low-cost index funds aligns perfectly with the strategy recommended for 80% of your portfolio (as discussed in Chapter 6).

Key Features for Teens:

Lowest Expense Ratios. Vanguard is famous for having some of the lowest expense ratios (the fee funds charge to operate) in the entire industry. When you are investing for 50+ years, even tiny fee differences add up to massive savings.

Index Fund Focus. Vanguard invented the index fund. Their platform makes it incredibly easy to find and invest in the exact index funds (like VTSAX or VTI) that form the core of a successful long-term strategy.

Zero Commission Trading. They offer commission-free trading on stocks and Vanguard ETFs.

Ideal for: The disciplined investor who intends to follow the "set-it-and-forget-it" model, prioritizing low fees and passive investing over frequent trading or deep individual stock research.

COMPARATIVE SNAPSHOT

Feature	**Fidelity**	**Charles Schwab**	**Vanguard**
Commissions (Stocks/ETFs)	$0	$0	$0

Custodial Account	Yes (UGMA/ UTMA & Youth Account)	Yes (UGMA/ UTMA)	Yes (UGMA/ UTMA)
Fractional Shares	Yes (Excellent)	Yes	Yes
Mobile App Rating	Excellent/ Modern	Very Good/ Professional	Good/ Functional
Best For	All-around starter and active learning	Research and stability	Long-term, low-cost index investing

The bottom line: Choose the platform that your custodian is most comfortable with, but if you have a choice, Fidelity offers the best overall experience for the teen who is starting from scratch and wants the freedom of fractional shares.

THE 'PARENT TRAP' INVESTMENT ACCOUNT: HOW TO GET YOUR FIRST $1,000 INVESTED LEGALLY (THE UGMA/UTMA PLAYBOOK)

THINK OF THE UGMA OR UTMA ACCOUNT AS YOUR NECESSARY COPILOT. You, the investor, are legally too young to sit in the pilot seat (i.e., sign the binding contracts that brokerages require). So, you need a trusted adult to be the designated driver until you turn the legal age.

This system is governed by either the Uniform Gifts to Minors Act (UGMA) or the Uniform Transfers to Minors Act (UTMA). You don't need to memorize the names; just know that they are the legal framework that lets people under the age of 18 (or 21 in some states) own investment assets.

WHY YOU CAN'T JUST OPEN A REGULAR ACCOUNT

THE PROBLEM IS SIMPLE: LEGALLY, YOU ARE A MINOR. FINANCIAL firms, brokerage houses, and banks require clients to be of the age of majority (usually 18) to enter into a contract. If you buy stock, you are entering a contract. Since you cannot legally sign that contract, you need an adult to do it for you.

The UGMA/UTMA account solves this by creating a legal container. It is set up under the adult's Social Security number and name, designated "as custodian for [Your Name]." Crucially, the account's assets are irrevocably held for your benefit. This leads us to the most important distinction in this setup: the two-player system.

PLAYER 1: THE CUSTODIAN (THE ADULT MANAGER)

THE CUSTODIAN IS THE ADULT WHO OPENS THE ACCOUNT (USUALLY a parent or guardian). They are the legal keyholder. Their responsibilities are serious and defined by law.

1. The Gatekeeper: They are the only person legally allowed to execute trades, link bank accounts, and handle transfers.

2. The Fiduciary: This is a fancy legal term meaning they must act solely in your best financial interest. They cannot use the money in the account for their own benefit, nor can they invest it in wildly speculative assets that no responsible adult would choose (though "responsible" is loosely defined when you're 16 and aggressively growth-focused!).

3. The Paperwork Czar: They handle all tax forms (like the 1099, which we'll discuss later) and administrative overhead.

The Custodian's job is management and execution. They are the hands that move the money, but they are not the brain.

PLAYER 2: THE BENEFICIAL OWNER (YOU, THE TEEN INVESTOR)

THIS IS YOU. YOU ARE THE SOLE, IRREVOCABLE OWNER OF EVERY SINGLE asset in that account, from the first share of index funds to the last $5 in cash. The ownership is the most powerful part of this account structure.

1. Irrevocable Ownership: Once money goes into a UGMA/UTMA, it belongs to you forever. Even if your parents get divorced, change their mind, or decide they need that money for something else, they cannot legally take it back. It is your property.

2. Strategic Control: While your adult must place the trade, in the context of this book, you are the chief investment strategist. You do the research (Chapter 5), you determine the allocation (Chapter 6), and you tell your Custodian which button to click.

3. The Automatic Transfer: This is the "graduation day" of your investing career. On a specific date (usually your 18th or 21st birthday, depending on your state of residence), the custodian's role vanishes. The assets are automatically transferred entirely into an account under your name and social security number. You become the sole manager, the sole owner, and the sole decision-maker.

THE KEY ADVANTAGE: IMMEDIATE, IRREVOCABLE OWNERSHIP

WHY GO THROUGH THIS LEGAL HASSLE? BECAUSE UNLIKE A 529 College Savings Plan (which has many rules about when and how the money can be used), the UGMA/UTMA money can be used for anything that benefits the minor—a car, college, a down payment on a house, or even that ridiculously expensive gaming PC you've been eyeing.

The most important thing to grasp is that the UGMA/UTMA account gives you ownership now. It forces the legal system to acknowledge that the money you are working to earn and invest is legitimately yours, and it starts the engine of compounding interest decades before your peers even open their first bank statement.

For the purpose of executing the 7-Day Wealth Launchpad (Chapters 6 and 7), your primary job is to secure a Custodian who is willing to take instruction from you on investment choices. Once you have that agreement, you have the Vault Key to your financial future.

——★–★–★——

THE ANTI-SCAMMER CHECKLIST: 7 CRITICAL SECURITY STEPS TO PROTECT YOUR PORTFOLIO FROM DIGITAL THIEVES

When you open a brokerage account, you are essentially opening a digital vault full of money. In the digital age, being financially savvy means being cyber-savvy. Since most of your investing will happen online, you need to treat your investment login credentials with the seriousness you'd treat your wallet—or your life savings.

Digital thieves are not looking for the biggest accounts; they are looking for the easiest ones to crack. By following this seven-step checklist, you will raise your security defences far above average, protecting your portfolio from unauthorized access and scams.

1. THE UNIQUE, IRONCLAD PASSWORD MANDATE

Your gaming logins, social media passwords, and your investment password should never be the same. Ever. If a hacker breaches your favorite streaming service, they immediately try those credentials on banking and brokerage sites. Your investment account requires an extremely strong, unique password (minimum 16 characters, combining upper and lower case, numbers, and symbols). If you can't remember them all, use a reputable password manager (like 1Password or LastPass) to generate and store them securely.

2. TWO-FACTOR AUTHENTICATION (2FA) IS MANDATORY

Two-Factor Authentication (sometimes called MFA or Multi-Factor Authentication) is the single most important barrier between a hacker and your money. 2FA means that even if a thief steals your password, they still need a second verification code, usually sent to your phone, to log in.

Set up 2FA immediately. Go one step further: if your brokerage offers it, use an authenticator app (like Google Authenticator or Authy) rather than relying on SMS text messages for codes. Text messages can sometimes be intercepted via advanced techniques, while app-based codes are far more secure.

3. MASTER THE ART OF PHISHING DEFENCE

Phishing scams are attempts to trick you into giving away personal information (passwords, social security numbers) via email or text. A common trick is an email that looks exactly like it came from your brokerage, claiming "suspicious activity detected, click here to verify your account."

Never click a link in an email concerning your money. Instead, close the email, and navigate directly to your brokerage's official website by typing the URL yourself. Your brokerage firm will never ask you to verify a password, Social Security number, or account number via email. Look closely at the sender's email address—it is often slightly misspelled (e.g., "FidelitySupport@gmail.com").

4. BEWARE THE 'TOO GOOD TO BE TRUE' INVESTMENT PITCH

This is perhaps the most critical protection against financial scams, not just digital ones. If an investment pitch, ad, or tip promises massive, guaranteed returns in a very short amount of time—run.

Real investing is slow, boring, and compounding. It grows over years and decades. Scams, often known as "pump and dumps" or pyramid schemes, rely on hype, pressure, and guaranteed high returns (think 50% in a month). If a stranger online (or even an acquaintance) tells you they know a secret stock that is about to explode, or asks you to send them crypto to invest on your behalf, it is a scam 100% of the time.

5. KEEP YOUR DEVICES AND SOFTWARE UPDATED

Cybercriminals exploit loopholes in old operating systems and outdated browser software. Think of software updates as immunization shots for your device. If your computer, phone, or tablet is running an old version of iOS, Android, or Windows, you are operating with known security vulnerabilities. Always accept and install critical software updates promptly, especially on the devices you use to access your financial accounts.

6. LOCK DOWN PUBLIC ACCESS POINTS

Never, under any circumstances, log into your investment account using public Wi-Fi (like at a coffee shop, airport, or school library). These networks can be easily monitored by others. Similarly, do not access your brokerage account on shared computers. If you absolutely must access your account on a public network, use a Virtual Private Network (VPN) for encrypted protection.

7. DON'T POST YOUR WINS ONLINE

The urge to brag about a big win or a rising portfolio balance is high, especially on social media platforms like TikTok, Discord, or Instagram. Resist this urge completely. Posting screenshots of your portfolio balance or, worse, your account statements, makes you an immediate target. It tells digital thieves exactly how much money you have and signals that you are a person worth trying to steal from. Keep your financial success private.

THE 14-MINUTE ACCOUNT SETUP: YOUR ZERO-FRICTION CHECKLIST TO FUNDING YOUR VERY FIRST TRADE

You've done the research, chosen your brokerage platform, and convinced your custodian (the adult) that this is a brilliant idea. Now, it's time to move from theory to execution.

This is the fastest 14 minutes of paperwork you will ever do. We are going to bypass the typical financial friction and get straight to the funding stage. You need to complete this checklist with your custodian present or with all of their information and authorization available.

PHASE I: PRE-LAUNCH MISSION CONTROL (0 - 5 MINUTES)

BEFORE YOU EVEN CLICK "OPEN ACCOUNT," YOU NEED A STACK OF documents ready. This phase takes the longest because nobody wants to pause mid-application to hunt for a Social Security card.

Required Documents (Minor Investor - You):

1. Social Security Number (SSN): Required for tax reporting purposes.

2. Date of Birth and Current Address: Must match any existing identification.

Required Documents (Custodian - The Adult):

1. Social Security Number (SSN): Required to open the custodial account.

2. Driver's License or State ID: Needed for verification and identity checks.

3. Current Bank Account Information: The routing and account number for the bank account you will use to fund the investment account (this is usually the custodian's account or a joint account).

PHASE II: THE APPLICATION SPRINT (5 - 10 MINUTES)

MOST MAJOR BROKERAGES (LIKE THE ONES WE REVIEWED IN THE LAST section) have streamlined this process. It should be entirely digital.

Step 1: Initiate the Account Opening

Navigate to your chosen brokerage platform (e.g., Fidelity, Schwab, etc.) and look for a large button that says "Open an Account" or "Get Started."

Step 2: Choose the Correct Account Type

This is the most critical step. Do NOT choose a standard taxable brokerage account. You must select:

Custodial Account

UGMA (Uniform Gifts to Minors Act) or UTMA (Uniform Transfers to Minors Act)

Note: The brokerage will default to the appropriate one based on your state.

Step 3: Enter Custodian Details (The Adult)

Because the adult is the legal fiduciary, their information goes in first. Input their full name, address, SSN, date of birth, and employment information (required by law). The system will usually verify their identity instantly.

Step 4: Enter Minor Investor Details (You)

Now, input your personal information, including your SSN and date of birth. The system establishes the legal link between the custodian and the beneficial owner (you).

Step 5: E-Sign and Submit

Review the summary page carefully. The custodian will need to read and digitally sign the application. Once submitted, the brokerage usually confirms account creation within minutes. You will receive an account number.

PHASE III: THE FUNDING FINISH LINE (10 - 14 MINUTES)

THE ACCOUNT IS OPEN! BUT AN EMPTY ACCOUNT DOESN'T BUY shares. It's time to send in the funds.

Step 6: Connect Your Funding Source

Go to the "Funding," "Transfers," or "Deposit" section of your new brokerage dashboard. You have two main options:

Instant Verification (Recommended): The brokerage uses a third-party service (like Plaid) to instantly and securely verify the login credentials for your bank account. This is fast and secure.

Manual Verification: You manually input the bank's Routing Number and your Account Number. The brokerage will typically send two tiny deposits (e.g., $0.11 and $0.23) to your bank account, and you must return to the brokerage platform 1-2 days later to confirm those amounts.

Step 7: Initiate Your First Deposit

Once the bank account is linked, you can initiate your first transfer. Choose the amount you wish to start with (remember: even $10 is enough if the platform supports fractional shares!) and confirm the transfer.

Total Time Elapsed: Approximately 14 Minutes.

What Happens Next?

It usually takes 1 to 3 business days for the funds to settle in your brokerage account. The money will show up as a "cash balance" ready to be deployed. Once the cash is settled, you are officially ready to place your first trade, which we will detail in Chapter 7. Congratulations—you have taken the most important step in your financial life!

CHAPTER FOUR

THE INVESTMENT ZOO: WHICH CREATURES GET YOU MASSIVE GROWTH (AND WHICH ONES KEEP YOU SAFE FROM PREDATORS)

WELCOME TO THE INVESTMENT ZOO.

Up until this point, we've focused on gathering your money, setting your goals, and getting the cage ready (your brokerage account). Now, it's time to decide which creatures you're actually going to put inside.

The financial world throws around dozens of complex names for investment vehicles—futures, options, commodities, derivatives—but you can ignore 95% of them. For a smart beginner, especially a young person focused on long-term wealth, the zoo contains only three main animals you need to domesticate: Stocks, Funds (ETFs/Index Funds), and Bonds.

Understanding these three categories—how they grow and how they crash—is the essential difference between a confident investor and someone just throwing darts at a board.

Think of it this way:

1. Stocks are the Cheetahs: They are fast, sleek, and can deliver massive results (high growth). But they are also solitary and vulnerable (high risk).

2. Funds are the Herds of Buffalo: They move together, protect each other, and reliably travel great distances (steady, diversified growth). They are resilient (moderate risk).

3. Bonds are the Tortoises: They are slow, steady, and focused purely on survival (low growth, but high safety). They are your protection from predators (low risk).

Let's meet these creatures one by one.

HOW TO GET NETFLIX AND APPLE TO PAY YOU: THE POWER OF BECOMING AN OWNER, NOT JUST A CUSTOMER

IMAGINE YOUR FAVOURITE VIDEO GAME. LET'S SAY IT'S MADE BY A huge company like Nintendo or Epic Games. When you buy the game, you are a customer. You give them money, and they give you a product. That's the end of the transaction.

Now, imagine you could own a tiny, miniature, fractional piece of Nintendo or Epic Games itself. Not just the game, but the actual company that makes the decisions, designs the consoles, and collects the billions in profits.

That is exactly what a stock is.

A stock (or a "share") represents proportional ownership in a corporation. If the company is worth $100 billion, and you own one millionth of that company, you own one millionth of the profits, the assets, and the future growth.

Why does this matter?

When you bought the video game, your wealth went down. When you buy the company's stock, your wealth is tied directly to the company's success. If the company makes an incredible new console and their profits triple, the value of your tiny slice of ownership (your stock) also triples.

When people talk about the "stock market," they are talking about the vast, worldwide marketplace where these shares of ownership are bought and sold.

The two main ways you make money from owning stocks are:

1. Capital Appreciation (The Growth): This is when the price of the stock goes up. If you bought one share of Apple for $50 and the company does well, ten years later that same share might be worth $250. That $200 increase is your capital appreciation. This is the main focus for young investors.

2. Dividends (The Payout): Some mature, profitable companies (like Coca-Cola or Microsoft) decide to share a small portion of their profits with their owners (shareholders). They literally send cash directly to your brokerage account, typically every three months. This is money you earn just for owning the stock. This is the ultimate "getting paid while you sleep" feature.

If you're deciding whether a stock is a good choice, ask yourself two simple questions:

Will this company be bigger in ten years? (Think Amazon, Google, Tesla.)

Will this company get knocked out by competition in the near future? (Think old technologies or businesses that haven't evolved.)

Stocks are vital for growth because historically, they are the single greatest generator of wealth. But remember the Cheetah analogy: they are fast and volatile. If you own a single stock and that company releases a product that fails, or a CEO makes a bad decision, your investment could plummet overnight. This is why we don't put all our money in one place.

The Lazy Genius Strategy: Investing in 500 Companies Simultaneously With One Single Click (The S&P 500 Secret)

If single stocks are the high-risk, high-reward Cheetahs, then Funds are the massive, defensive herds.

A fund is simply a giant basket that holds dozens, hundreds, or even thousands of different stocks and/or bonds. When you buy one share of the fund, you instantly own a tiny piece of everything inside the basket.

Funds are the ultimate lazy genius strategy because they solve the biggest problem with single stocks: volatility. If one company in your fund goes bankrupt, it might be balanced out by the 999 other successful companies in the basket, barely affecting your overall return. This is the power of diversification.

There are two major types of funds you need to know:

1. Mutual Funds: These are professionally managed baskets of investments. You buy them based on their Net Asset Value (NAV) once per day. They often have high fees and are less flexible, which is why we generally skip them unless you have specialized retirement accounts later on.

2. Exchange-Traded Funds (ETFs): These are the modern, superior version for beginners. An ETF acts exactly like a stock—you can buy and sell shares of the fund anytime the market is open—but instead of holding one company, it holds the basket of assets. They usually have extremely low fees.

The greatest wealth-building tool available to a beginner investor is the Index Fund (which is usually packaged as an ETF).

An index is a list of companies. The most famous one is the S&P 500. This index tracks the performance of 500 of the largest, most successful publicly traded companies in the United States (Apple, Microsoft, Google, etc.).

An S&P 500 Index Fund (often labeled with tickers like VOO or FXAIX) simply owns small slices of all 500 companies in that index.

Think of the S&P 500 as the "scorecard" for the overall US economy. Historically, over any 20-year period, the S&P 500 has never failed to deliver positive returns, averaging about 10% per year before inflation.

When you buy an S&P 500 Index Fund, you are essentially betting on the enduring strength of the entire American economy—not just one CEO or one product launch. For your core portfolio (the 70-80% safety net we will discuss in Chapter 6), Index Funds are non-negotiable. They are reliable, low-cost, and require zero research.

The key takeaway? Index Funds allow you to participate in massive growth while substantially lowering your risk profile. They are the bedrock of any successful long-term portfolio.

—★-★-★—

WHEN TO EMBRACE BORING: DEPLOYING YOUR 'EMERGENCY BRAKES' WHEN THE STOCK MARKET GOES WILD

So far, we have the fast-moving growth engine (Stocks) and the highly reliable backbone (Index Funds). Now we need the ultimate safety net: the assets that preserve your cash when everything else is shaking. These are your Tortoises.

The stock market is cyclical. It goes up, and sometimes it goes down sharply (these are called corrections or crashes). When the stock market crashes, you need assets that hold their value or even go up while stocks are falling.

MEET BONDS AND CERTIFICATES OF DEPOSIT (CDS).

Bonds are essentially loans. When you buy a bond, you are lending your money to an entity (usually a government, like the US Treasury, or a very large corporation) for a fixed period of time. In return, they promise to pay you interest every year, and pay back the principal amount when the bond "matures."

Stocks: You own a piece of the company's future profits (unpredictable).

Bonds: You are a creditor. They owe you money (predictable, fixed return).

Because bonds guarantee a payout (unless the entity goes bankrupt, which is rare for the US government), they are far less volatile than stocks. Their returns are much lower (often 3% to 5% annually), but they serve a crucial role: stability. When the stock market is crashing because investors are scared, they tend to pull money out of stocks and put it into safe assets like government bonds. This stability is why they are sometimes called "fixed income."

For a young investor, your portfolio will likely hold very few bonds—perhaps only 5% to 10%—because you are focused on maximizing growth, and bonds hold growth back. However, they are essential knowledge for when you need a place to safely stash money you might need in the near future (e.g., college tuition in four years).

Certificates of Deposit (CDs) are even more boring. A CD is a promise you make to a bank to leave a lump sum of money deposited for a specific period (e.g., 6 months, 2 years, 5 years). In exchange, the bank gives you a slightly higher interest rate than a standard savings account. They are extremely low-risk, as they are insured by the government (FDIC), but they offer virtually no growth potential compared to stocks. They are excellent, however, for short-term savings where preserving capital is your top priority.

THE CRYPTO TRAP AND FRACTIONAL PROPERTY: WARNING SIGNS AND WHEN TO AVOID HIGH-STAKES ASSETS

WHILE THE CORE OF YOUR PORTFOLIO SHOULD LIVE WITHIN THE safety of the three creatures above, it's impossible to talk about modern investing without mentioning the wild, unregulated section of the zoo: Alternative Assets.

These investments are called "alternative" because they don't follow the typical rules of the stock market. The two most popular (and most dangerous for beginners) are Cryptocurrency and Fractional Real Estate.

1. THE SIREN SONG OF CRYPTO

CRYPTOCURRENCY (LIKE BITCOIN AND ETHEREUM) IS DIGITAL CURrency secured by cryptography. It promises to be a global, decentralized replacement for traditional money and banking systems.

The potential for quick, life-changing gains in crypto has lured millions of young investors. And yes, people have gotten very rich, very fast.

However, crypto is the ultimate high-stakes gamble for a beginner. It is highly volatile, meaning its value can shoot up 40% one week and drop 60% the next. There is no underlying government or corporate entity to back it up, making it extremely speculative. Its value is driven almost entirely by hype, emotion, and future potential, not existing profits (like a stock).

The Cautionary Rule: If you are determined to invest in crypto, only allocate money you are 100% prepared to lose. This is often called "play money" or "fun money." Keep this allocation minuscule—perhaps 1% to 5% of your total investment capital. Your focus must remain on the long-term, proven growth vehicles: Index Funds. Don't let the promise of a quick 10x return distract you from the certainty of a 10x return over 20 years.

2. FRACTIONAL REAL ESTATE

REAL ESTATE (BUYING HOUSES OR APARTMENTS) IS A HISTORIC PATH to wealth, but buying an entire house is usually impossible for a teenager. Fractional real estate platforms allow you to buy small slices of property.

The benefit is that real estate historically holds its value well and provides rental income. The drawback is that it's usually illiquid (hard to sell quickly), involves high fees, and these specialized fractional platforms often add layers of complexity and risk for the novice.

The Beginner's Verdict: Real estate should be considered once your stock portfolio is substantial (>$50,000) and you understand the market deeply. For now, the complexity and low liquidity of fractional property make it a distraction from your core mission.

YOUR STRATEGY: THE 90/10 RULE

YOUR FIRST INVESTMENT STRATEGY SHOULD BE RUTHLESSLY SIMPLE and focused on maximum time advantage.

90% of your money goes into the reliable, diversified herd (Index Funds). This is your long-term, non-negotiable wealth generator.

10% of your money goes into the exciting, high-risk Cheetahs (Individual Stocks). This is where you practice your research skills from Chapter 5, and where you allow for massive, yet controlled, upside.

By understanding the basic functions and risks of these foundational creatures, you have successfully completed the tour of the Investment Zoo and are ready to start buying.

HOW TO GET NETFLIX AND APPLE TO PAY YOU: THE POWER OF BECOMING AN OWNER, NOT JUST A CUSTOMER

You spend $15 a month on Netflix. You probably buy a new pair of Nike sneakers every six months. If you're a gamer, you've dumped serious cash into microtransactions on Fortnite or perhaps pre-ordered the latest console release from Microsoft or Sony.

You, dear reader, are a fantastic customer. You are the engine of corporate profit.

Here's the massive mindset shift that turns customers into investors: Stop simply funding the companies you love. Start owning them.

When you invest, you change your relationship with these giants. Instead of your money flowing out of your wallet and into theirs, you set up a system where their profits flow back to you.

This is the power of the stock.

WHAT EXACTLY IS A STOCK?

Imagine your favorite tech company, let's call it "Global Mega Corp" (but think Apple, Amazon, or Google). Global Mega Corp is worth trillions of dollars. If you wanted to start a company that big, you'd need billions of dollars, right?

When companies are looking to raise massive amounts of capital—money they need to build new factories, launch new products, or expand globally—they don't typically go asking just one bank. They sell ownership in the company to the public.

A stock is simply a tiny, fractional piece of ownership in a publicly traded company. When you purchase a share of Netflix, you literally become a part-owner of the company that streams Stranger Things and Squid Game to 250 million users worldwide.

You aren't buying a product; you are buying equity.

When you buy a share (which is the technical term for a single unit of stock), you are betting on that company's future success. If Apple releases a ground-breaking new VR headset, or if Microsoft dominates the gaming market, the company becomes more valuable. And since you own a piece of it, your piece also becomes more valuable.

THE STOCK EXCHANGE: THE GLOBAL GARAGE SALE

So where do you actually buy this slice of Apple or this fraction of Netflix? You buy them on the stock exchange.

Forget the image of people yelling and throwing paper on a trading floor. Today, the stock exchange is a massive, highly regulated, and extremely fast digital marketplace (like NASDAQ or the New York Stock Exchange). This is the place where investors and traders buy and sell shares of public companies.

When you place a trade through your brokerage app (which we will set up in Chapter 3), you are simply submitting an order to this exchange. If you want to buy 10 shares of the popular gaming company Roblox, the exchange instantly finds someone willing to sell 10 shares of Roblox at the current market price and executes the transfer.

The beautiful part? You don't need to know who the seller is, and they don't need to know you. The exchange handles the messy parts.

How Ownership Pays Off (Dividends and Growth)

There are two primary ways that stocks generate wealth for you over the long term, and neither requires you to lift a finger once you've placed the trade.

1. CAPITAL APPRECIATION (THE GROWTH):

This is the main event. If you buy one share of Nvidia (a leading chipmaker for AI and gaming) for $100 today, and over the next five years, they keep dominating the chip market, that share might be worth $300. That $200 increase in value is called capital appreciation. You haven't sold the stock yet, but the value of your asset has increased because the company is performing well. This is why you need to choose stocks in companies you believe will be more successful a decade from now than they are today.

2. DIVIDENDS (THE PASSIVE PAYCHECK):

Some, but not all, mature companies—think Coca-Cola, Starbucks, or utility companies—have so much extra cash flowing in that they decide to share a portion of their profits directly with their shareholders. This payout is called a dividend.

Dividends are often paid out quarterly (every three months). If you own 100 shares of Coca-Cola, and they pay a dividend of $0.50 per share, you would receive $50 deposited directly into your brokerage account that quarter.

The best part about dividends is that they are totally passive income. You literally get paid just for being an owner. Many investors choose to automatically use those dividends to buy more shares of the company, further accelerating the compounding effect (remember the snowball from Chapter 1?).

THE ULTIMATE INVESTMENT: TIME

WHEN YOU START INVESTING AS A TEENAGER, YOU ARE NOT FOCUSED on quick profits; you are focused on locking in ownership for the next 10, 20, or 40 years.

The most successful investors didn't pick every single winning stock; they simply identified good companies and held onto them for decades, allowing the companies' success and the magic of compounding to do the heavy lifting.

The key takeaway is this: Every time you buy a product from a major corporation, ask yourself, "Do I also own a piece of this company?" If the answer is no, you are leaving money on the table. Your money should be invested in companies whose products and services you use every day, transforming you from a loyal customer into a successful owner.

THE LAZY GENIUS STRATEGY: INVESTING IN 500 COMPANIES SIMULTANEOUSLY WITH ONE SINGLE CLICK (THE S&P 500 SECRET)

IMAGINE FOR A MOMENT YOU HAD TO BUILD THE ULTIMATE SPORTS team, but you could only pick one player. If that player got hurt, your whole season is over. That's what buying a single stock is like. It's high-risk, high-reward, and extremely stressful.

The Lazy Genius Strategy is about making your portfolio resilient. We want a team of 500 superstar players working for you, so if one has a bad day, the others carry the load. This is called diversification, and it's arguably the single most important concept in long-term investing.

How do you buy 500 companies without having to research 500 annual reports? You don't. You buy a fund.

A fund is simply a massive collection of assets—stocks, bonds, etc.—that has been professionally packaged into a single investment product. When you buy one share of the fund, you are purchasing tiny slivers of every asset inside that package. It's the ultimate investment two-for-one deal.

THE S&P 500 SECRET: INSTANT DIVERSIFICATION

THE SIMPLEST, MOST EFFECTIVE, AND HISTORICALLY PROVEN method of investing is using an Index Fund that tracks the S&P 500.

What is the S&P 500? It stands for the Standard & Poor's 500. It is an index that tracks the performance of the 500 largest publicly traded companies in the United States. We're talking about the titans of industry: Apple, Microsoft, Amazon, Google, Tesla, Johnson & Johnson, Coca-Cola—the companies that effectively run the modern world.

When you buy a share in an S&P 500 Index Fund, you are not betting on one company; you are betting on the entire engine of American business.

This is the "Lazy Genius" part: If you invest $100 into an S&P 500 fund, you have instantly achieved a level of diversification that used to take professional money managers weeks to build. Your risk is dramatically lower than if you had put that same $100 into a single stock like GameStop.

For the vast majority of long-term investors, the S&P 500 is their best-performing asset. Why? Because the American economy, despite recessions and crises, has always trended up over the long run.

THE TWO FLAVORS OF FUNDS: ETF VS. MUTUAL FUND

WHEN YOU GO TO YOUR BROKERAGE APP, YOU WILL SEE FUNDS LISTED in two main structures: ETFs and Mutual Funds. They both hold baskets of stocks, but they behave differently when you buy them.

1. Exchange-Traded Funds (ETFs)

ETFs are the most modern and teen-friendly option.

How they work: They trade exactly like a stock. If you decide at 11:00 AM that you want to buy an ETF, you hit "buy," and the transaction executes immediately at the current market price.

Pros for Teens:

Low Minimums: You can often buy fractional shares of an ETF, meaning you can invest with as little as $5 or $10.

Flexibility: You can trade them easily throughout the day.

Low Costs: Most major S&P 500 ETFs have extremely low expense ratios (the fee the fund charges you yearly).

Example S&P 500 ETFs: VOO, SPY, IVV.

2. Mutual Funds

Mutual funds are the classic, older fund structure.

How they work: They do not trade throughout the day. When you place an order to buy a mutual fund, the transaction is executed only once, after the market closes at 4:00 PM (at the Net Asset Value price).

Pros for Teens:

Easy to Automate: They are excellent for setting up recurring, automatic purchases.

Cons for Teens:

High Minimums: Many mutual funds require an initial investment of $1,000 or $3,000, which is often too high for a beginner investor.

Example S&P 500 Mutual Funds: FXAIX, VFIAX. (Note: Fidelity and Vanguard often waive the minimums if you use their specific brokerage accounts, but the ETF route is generally simpler for starting out.)

THE BEGINNER'S BLUEPRINT: INDEX FUNDS ARE KING

For your first, foundational investments (which should make up the bulk of your portfolio, as you will see in Chapter 6), you should stick almost exclusively to low-cost Index Funds, specifically those tracking the S&P 500 or the Total U.S. Stock Market.

The index fund strategy is the opposite of day trading. It requires minimal monitoring, minimal research, and minimal stress. It leverages the growth of the largest companies in the world without making you reliant on any single one of them.

If you decide to buy VOO, you are now a shareholder in 500 of the world's most powerful companies. You have made the smart, lazy genius choice. You have done the work of a seasoned professional with one click.

—★-★-★—

WHEN TO EMBRACE BORING: DEPLOYING YOUR 'EMERGENCY BRAKES' WHEN THE STOCK MARKET GOES WILD

If Chapter 4 has felt like a high-octane lesson in rocket science, preparing you to launch your money to the moon, this section is about installing the emergency brakes.

When you're young, you can afford to be aggressive (as we discussed, time is your ultimate safety net). But even the most aggressive investor needs a stabilizer—something that won't plummet just because Elon Musk tweeted something controversial. That's where the boring, predictable assets come in.

These assets are the opposite of stocks. Stocks give you ownership and high growth potential; these assets give you stability and guaranteed—albeit minimal—returns. They are the shock absorbers for your portfolio.

BONDS: YOU ARE THE BANK

When you buy a stock, you become an owner (equity holder). When you buy a bond, you become a lender (debt holder).

A bond is simply a fancy IOU. You are loaning money to an entity—usually a major corporation (a Corporate Bond) or a government (a Treasury Bond). In exchange for your loan, the entity promises to do three things:

1. Pay you back the original amount (the principal) on a specific date (the maturity date).

2. Pay you regular interest payments (called the coupon) along the way.

Imagine your favorite massive gaming company needs $50 million to develop its next AAA title. Instead of selling more stock (and diluting the value of existing shares), they issue bonds. You buy $1,000 worth of their bonds. They now owe you that $1,000, and they will pay you maybe 4% interest every year until the bond matures.

Why bonds are boring (and why that's good):

Bonds are safer than stocks because debt holders (bond owners) legally get paid before equity holders (stock owners) if a company goes bankrupt. The company must pay its bond obligations first. Because they are much less volatile, bonds typically offer lower returns than stocks.

If the stock market is crashing and stocks are down 30%, bonds might only be down 5% (or, often, they might even be up, as investors rush to safety). This stabilizing effect is their superpower.

CERTIFICATES OF DEPOSIT (CDS): THE FINANCIAL TIME-OUT

While bonds are debt issued by corporations or governments, Certificates of Deposit (CDs) are the simplest and safest fixed-income product offered by banks.

Think of a CD as a locked savings account. You deposit a sum of money into the CD and agree to leave it there for a fixed period of time—say, 6 months, 1 year, or 5 years. In return for locking up your money, the bank guarantees you a specific, slightly higher interest rate than a standard savings account.

The major advantage of CDs is their rock-solid safety. In the US, CDs held at insured banks are protected by the FDIC (Federal Deposit Insurance Corporation) up to $250,000. This means that even if the bank completely collapses, your money is safe and guaranteed by the government.

The Trade-Off:

The trade-off for this extreme safety is liquidity and return. You usually cannot touch the money before the term expires without paying a penalty (low liquidity), and the interest rate is generally quite low compared to the potential growth of stocks.

Your Portfolio's Emergency Brakes

So, why does a young investor, focused entirely on growth, need these boring tools?

The primary reason is risk management and stability.

For a young investor with a 40+ year time horizon, your portfolio allocation should probably be 80-95% growth assets (stocks and index funds). But the remaining 5-20% allocated to safe, stable assets (bonds or CDs) serves two crucial functions:

1. Shock Absorption: When the inevitable market crash hits (and it will, multiple times over your lifetime), your stock assets will plummet. But your bonds and CDs will hold their value, cushioning the overall blow. This makes it easier to sleep at night and prevents you from panicking and selling everything.

2. Dry Powder: This is the most exciting function. When the stock market crashes, everything goes "on sale." If all your money is tied up in falling stocks, you can't buy the sales. However, if you have 10% of your portfolio safely tucked away in bonds that haven't dropped in value, you can sell those stable assets and use that money to buy highly discounted stocks.

In essence, bonds and CDs are your disciplined emergency fund within the investment world. They ensure that even when the stock market goes wild, you have cash that retains its value, ready to deploy for maximum profit when the dust settles. You embrace the boring stuff now so you can afford to buy the exciting stuff later.

THE CRYPTO TRAP AND FRACTIONAL PROPERTY: WARNING SIGNS AND WHEN TO AVOID HIGH-STAKES ASSETS

So far, we have focused on assets that have a long, proven track history of growth: stocks and bonds. These are the workhorses of the financial world. But when you are exploring the investment world, you inevitably hear about the shiny, new, and often loud things. These are the alternative assets, and while they hold immense future potential, they also carry immense risk—especially for new investors.

These alternative assets include things like cryptocurrency (Bitcoin, Ethereum, etc.), venture capital, collectibles (rare sneakers, art), and increasingly, fractional ownership of real estate or expensive art.

The fundamental distinction you must internalize is this: index funds and major stocks are investments, meaning they represent ownership in income-generating assets that have been rigorously tested for decades. Most alternative assets, especially for beginners, are pure speculation.

The key rule for a beginner is: Do not touch these assets until your foundational portfolio (index funds, blue-chip stocks) is 100% established and you are contributing to it regularly. If you feel compelled to experiment, dedicate only a tiny amount of money—money you are perfectly fine losing entirely.

THE CRYPTO TRAP: VOLATILITY IS NOT GROWTH

Cryptocurrency is often the first alternative asset that grabs a teen's attention, and for good reason. It's digital, it's exciting, and the headlines constantly scream about massive, life-changing gains.

At its core, cryptocurrency is a digital asset built on blockchain technology. While the technology itself is revolutionary and may underpin future financial systems, the digital coins themselves are highly volatile. They are not tied to the earnings or profits of a company (like a stock) or a stream of payments (like a bond). Their value is based almost entirely on hype, market sentiment, and speculation.

What this means in practice is that a specific cryptocurrency can surge 400% in a month and then drop 80% in the following week. For a young investor, seeing your initial $100 turn into $500 is exhilarating; seeing it crash back down to $50 is a catastrophic psychological experience that often leads to panic selling.

WARNING SIGNS: AVOID HIGH-STAKES SPECULATION

1. THE OVERNIGHT PROMISE: IF AN ASSET PROMISES TO MAKE YOU rich overnight or is promoted heavily by influencers with no financial background, it is a speculative trap.

2. Emotional Investing: Crypto is driven by "Fear of Missing Out" (FOMO). True investing is boring, calculated, and long-term. Crypto trading is rarely boring, which means it's rarely true investing.

3. Lack of Fundamentals: It is extremely difficult to determine the intrinsic value of a cryptocurrency. You cannot use the P/E ratio or quarterly earnings reports to judge if Bitcoin is cheap or expensive, making educated buying impossible.

For the beginner investor, your focus must be on maximizing the mathematical certainty of compounding, not gambling on volatile digital assets.

FRACTIONAL PROPERTY: THE LIQUIDITY QUESTION

ANOTHER RISING TREND IS FRACTIONAL OWNERSHIP. THIS INVOLVES buying a tiny, digital piece of an expensive, traditionally illiquid asset. The most common example is fractional real estate (buying 0.1% of an apartment building) or fractional ownership of expensive sports cars or fine art.

The Appeal: Real estate is traditionally a strong, reliable asset class that keeps pace with inflation. Fractional ownership makes it accessible to investors with only $100.

The Caution: While real estate is generally stable, the fractional market is not. When you buy a share of a fractional asset, you must consider the concept of liquidity. Liquidity refers to how easily and quickly you can sell an asset and convert it back to cash without losing value.

A stock in the S&P 500 is highly liquid; you can sell it in seconds during market hours. Fractional real estate, however, is often illiquid. There may not be an immediate buyer for your tiny share of the apartment building when you need cash. Furthermore, these platforms often carry high management fees, which eat into the already slow returns of real estate.

THE VERDICT ON ALTERNATIVES

ALTERNATIVE ASSETS ARE RESERVED FOR THE "PLAY MONEY" SEGment of an already diversified, robust portfolio. For a teen starting out, your initial focus must be on capital preservation and maximum growth through compounding—goals that are best achieved through low-cost index funds and a small selection of high-quality, dividend-paying stocks.

If you decide to dedicate a portion of your portfolio to these high-stakes assets, never exceed 5% of your total invested capital, and treat that 5% as tuition paid for learning about high-risk markets. Get rich slowly and safely before you consider gambling quickly.

CHAPTER FIVE

—★-★-★—

THE INSIDER'S LENS: HOW TO SPOT A 10X STOCK BEFORE WALL STREET EVEN NOTICES

Chapter 5 is where we transition from being good resource managers to being smart business analysts. Up until now, we've focused on the safety net—setting up the account, defining goals, and learning about foundational assets like index funds. That's the core of any stable portfolio.

But let's be real. Nobody ever got rich only owning boring index funds. Those funds provide the slow, steady grind that makes you comfortable. The 10X stocks—the companies that double, triple, or ten-times your money—are the ones that move the needle.

These 10X stocks are what you're hunting for when you dedicate the 20% to 40% of your portfolio to individual company stocks (as we'll discuss in Chapter 6).

To find them, you need an insider's lens. This doesn't mean knowing illegal secrets; it means learning how to see the world through the eyes of an investor, not just a customer. It means recognizing that the things you and your friends are already obsessed with might be the next Apple or Amazon.

Your Secret Weapon: Turning Your Daily Habits (Gaming, Streaming, Shopping) Into Investment Profits

The biggest lie about market research is that it requires a suit, a spreadsheet, and a corner office on Wall Street.

The truth? As a teenager, you have a massive, unfair advantage over the vast majority of professional investors who manage giant hedge funds: you are the early adopter. You are the consumer of the future.

While the 50-year-old analyst is busy reading quarterly reports about obsolete manufacturing processes, you are living the technological future right now. You were the one who understood the appeal of TikTok before it was a massive international trend. You know which gaming studio is dominating the conversation. You know which sneaker drop is the real deal and which one is already dead.

This is qualitative research, and it is gold. You don't need to read fancy reports; you need to formalize your own observations.

The goal here is to shift your perspective. Every time you open an app, buy a product, or use a subscription service, ask yourself three simple questions:

1. The Loyalty Question: How obsessed are people with this product? Is it just a temporary fad (like that one viral dance challenge), or is it ingrained into daily life? (Think about the difference between a new meme stock and Spotify—people are legitimately reliant on Spotify.) High loyalty means a high barrier to entry for competitors.

2. The Disruptor Question: Is this company making something radically better, cheaper, or faster than the established alternatives? (Think how Netflix disrupted Blockbuster, or how a specific gaming engine dominates graphics performance.) Look for businesses that simplify the user experience or entirely redefine a market.

3. The Moat Question: Does this company have a "moat" around its business? A moat is a unique advantage that makes it nearly impossible for competitors to steal their customers. This could be powerful brand recognition (like Nike), massive network effects (like Discord or Facebook), or patent protection (like pharmaceutical companies). A great investment has a deep, alligator-filled moat.

Let's look at a concrete example: You notice every streamer you follow is using a specific brand of specialized microphone or streaming software. That's not a coincidence. That's a signal that this particular piece of technology is becoming the industry standard. Your next step isn't to buy the product, but to check who owns the company and if they are publicly traded.

Your daily habits are your personal, real-time market research lab. Start a running list of companies you and your friends are genuinely excited about. These companies are your investment candidates.

THE 30-SECOND VALUATION TEST: INSTANTLY KNOWING IF A STOCK IS 'ON SALE' OR HUGELY OVERPRICED

Okay, you've used your insider lens and found Company X, which makes the revolutionary gaming console everyone will want next year. Great. But before you hit the "Buy" button, you need to answer a vital question: What is a fair price to pay?

Just because a company is amazing doesn't mean its stock is a good investment. Think of it like buying a collectible sneaker: if the shoe is awesome but the seller wants $5,000 for it, you probably shouldn't buy it, no matter how cool it is. It's overpriced.

To avoid buying fantastic companies at ridiculous prices, we use a simple tool called the Price-to-Earnings Ratio (P/E Ratio).

The P/E Ratio is the single most critical metric for a beginning investor. It is essentially asking: How much are investors willing to pay for every $1 the company earns?

The Formula:

P/E Ratio = (Current Stock Price) / (Annual Earnings Per Share)

If a stock trades at $100 and the company earned $5 per share over the last year, the P/E ratio is 20 ($100 / $5 = 20). This means investors are willing to pay $20 for every $1 of profit the company generates.

Here's the simple translation:

Low P/E (e.g., 8 to 15): The stock is typically considered "cheap" or "undervalued" relative to the money it's currently making. This can be a value investment, but beware: sometimes a stock has a low P/E because the market thinks the company's best days are behind it.

Moderate P/E (e.g., 15 to 25): This is generally considered "fairly valued." This range often tracks closely with the average P/E of the overall stock market (like the S&P 500).

High P/E (e.g., 30+): This means the stock is "expensive" based on current earnings. Investors are willing to pay a premium because they expect the company's earnings to explode in the future. You are paying for anticipated growth.

The 30-Second Test:

1. Look up the P/E ratio for your candidate stock. Your brokerage platform or any major financial news site (like Yahoo Finance) lists this number right on the company summary page.

2. Look up the P/E ratio for its closest competitor or its industry average.

3. Compare. Is your company's P/E 50, while its rival's is 20? If so, you are paying 2.5 times more for the future potential of your company. This doesn't mean it's a bad buy, but it means you need to be absolutely certain your growth projections are right. If that growth doesn't materialize, the stock price will plummet.

As a young growth investor, you will often lean toward stocks with a slightly higher P/E because you are hunting for companies that will grow rapidly. But always use the P/E ratio as your instant check to make sure you aren't paying an insane price for a company that hasn't earned it yet.

Ignoring 99% of Financial News: The 4 Key Macro-Drivers That ACTUALLY Move Your Money

If you turn on financial news during market hours, it sounds like the world is either ending or entering a new golden age, all within the span of one commercial break. Analysts scream about trivial daily movements, and the overall feeling is chaos.

This is noise, and it is a productivity killer. Your job as a long-term investor is to filter out 99% of that daily noise and focus only on the few big, slow-moving macro-drivers that genuinely impact the economy over years, not hours.

Think of it this way: the stock price of an individual company (like a new video game developer) might drop 3% because a reviewer gave them a 7/10 score. That's noise. But if the entire stock market drops 10% across the board, that's usually because one of the following four economic levers has been pulled.

These are the only four financial topics you need to occasionally check in on:

1. THE COST OF MONEY (INTEREST RATES)

This is the most powerful lever in the modern economy, controlled primarily by the U.S. Federal Reserve (often called "The Fed").

When the Fed raises interest rates, it means banks must charge more for loans. Suddenly, it costs more for companies to borrow money to build new factories, launch new products, or hire new workers. This slows down growth. For growth stocks, which rely heavily on cheap, borrowed money, rising rates are usually very bad news. When The Fed signals rates are going up, growth stocks generally fall.

When The Fed lowers interest rates, money is cheap and plentiful. Companies borrow freely, invest heavily, and grow fast. This is usually great for stocks.

Action: Don't watch the minute-to-minute speculation about the Fed. Wait for their official announcements about rates, and understand the general direction of travel (Are rates rising or falling?).

—★–★–★—

2. INFLATION

INFLATION IS THE RATE AT WHICH THE GENERAL PRICE OF GOODS and services is rising. If you notice your favorite energy drink costs 20 cents more this week than last week, that's inflation in action.

High inflation is a headache for businesses because their costs for materials, shipping, and labor all increase. If a company can't raise its prices fast enough to keep up, its profit margins shrink. This makes their stock less attractive. On the flip side, some companies (like those owning hard assets, such as real estate or raw materials) tend to do better during high inflation.

3. STRUCTURAL TECHNOLOGY SHIFTS (THE TSUNAMI)

THIS IS THE LONG GAME. YOU ARE LOOKING FOR CHANGES SO MASSIVE they redefine the economy. Think about the rise of the internet in the 90s, the smartphone in the 2000s, or AI in the 2020s.

When these tsunamis hit, they create opportunities for new, 10X companies, and they also kill off old ones. As an investor, you need to identify the enabling technologies (e.g., semiconductors, cloud computing services) that all the subsequent innovators will have to use.

4. GOVERNMENT SPENDING AND REGULATION

Government policy creates winners and losers. If the government announces massive spending on infrastructure, the companies that make cement, steel, and construction equipment will likely win. If the government announces strict new environmental regulations, the companies leading in renewable energy technology will benefit, while heavy polluters may suffer.

Your job is to read headlines about these four drivers, understand their direction, and then go back to your day-to-day life.

SHOCKING TRUTH: WHY CHECKING YOUR PORTFOLIO EVERY DAY GUARANTEES YOU'LL LOSE MONEY

If you have ever been told that you should check your stock portfolio every morning to make sure everything is okay, you were given terrible advice.

In fact, if you check your portfolio daily, you are dramatically increasing your chances of making emotional mistakes that will sabotage your long-term returns.

This sounds counterintuitive, so let me explain why daily checks are a financial trap:

THE SHORT-TERM MARKET IS RANDOM

If you look at the stock market over 20 years, it's a beautiful upward sloping line (even with some terrifying dips). If you look at the market over 20 minutes, it's a chaotic, nonsensical mess driven by algorithms, rumors, and momentary panics.

When you check your portfolio daily, you are focusing entirely on the noise. You are magnifying the tiny, irrelevant daily fluctuations. A 1% drop in the value of your portfolio might make you feel terrible and trigger an emotional response like, "Oh no, I need to sell before it gets worse!"

This is the primary way investors lose money: by selling good investments during temporary dips.

THE MYTH OF DAY TRADING

Many new investors—especially tech-savvy young people—get sucked into the excitement of day trading (buying and selling stocks rapidly within the same day or week). They see a few wins and think they can beat the market.

The statistical reality is brutal: Over 90% of day traders lose money. The people who make money are the institutional traders with high-frequency algorithms, supercomputers, and zero emotion. You are bringing a BB gun to a thermonuclear war.

This book is about investing—the act of owning a piece of a great business for a long time. It is not about trading—the act of guessing which way a stock will move next week.

THE TIME ADVANTAGE

You have the single most powerful weapon in the financial world: time. A 1% dip today doesn't matter if your company grows 500% over the next 15 years.

Your strategy must be boring:

1. Research thoroughly (using the steps above).

2. Buy great companies or broad funds regularly (Dollar-Cost Averaging, which we will cover soon).

3. Ignore the day-to-day drama.

We recommend checking your portfolio monthly, or even better, quarterly. This allows you to check for rebalancing (making sure your ratios haven't shifted too far) and to assess long-term performance, not short-term noise.

Remember: The stock market is designed to transfer wealth from the impatient to the patient. Be patient.

—★-★-★—

YOUR SECRET WEAPON: TURNING YOUR DAILY HABITS (GAMING, STREAMING, SHOPPING) INTO INVESTMENT PROFITS

Wall Street is an echo chamber. It's filled with people who often live in a bubble, analyzing spreadsheets while completely missing the cultural shifts happening right outside their highly polished windows. They spend weeks researching if a new product is successful, pouring over consumer reports and trying to interview "experts."

But you? You already know.

Your daily life—the apps you use, the clothes you buy, the games you stream, the services you rely on to procrastinate on homework—is the fastest, most powerful market research tool available. You are the early adopter. You are the prime consumer. You are, in effect, an insider.

Your secret weapon as a young investor is leveraging this knowledge to spot winning companies before the establishment catches on.

THE CONSUMER-TO-INVESTOR PIPELINE

Becoming a savvy investor doesn't mean memorizing quarterly reports; it means asking three simple questions every time you encounter a product or service you love:

1. Is this successful? (Is everyone talking about it? Are my friends using it constantly?)

2. Is this sticky? (Is it a fleeting trend, or is it something I now rely on? For instance, buying one pair of trendy shoes is a fad; needing Microsoft Office or Amazon Prime is sticky.)

3. Who is getting paid? (Which publicly traded company owns this product or service?)

This process turns passive consumption into active analysis.

GAMING: ANALYZING THE MICRO-TRANSACTION GOLD RUSH

Let's look at gaming. A traditional analyst might see an income statement from a massive developer like Electronic Arts (EA) or Take-Two Interactive (TTWO). They see high revenue, but they don't understand why.

You know why. You know the difference between a game that fades after launch and a game that dominates the ecosystem for years through continuous content drops and, critically, micro-transactions.

If a game is successful at selling digital items—skins, battle passes, seasonal content—that isn't just "extra money"; it's pure profit with minimal manufacturing cost. When you see your entire friend group willing to shell out $10 for a new character skin in a free-to-play game, you aren't just looking at an impulse purchase; you are witnessing a reliable, recurring revenue stream.

Action Step: Instead of just buying the skin, identify the parent company and research its stock. Are the revenue numbers growing thanks to this highly successful monetization model? If the answer is yes, you've spotted a profit engine.

SHOPPING AND TRENDS: THE POWER OF STATUS

LOOK AT THE PHYSICAL GOODS YOU AND YOUR PEERS PRIORITIZE. IN the mid-2010s, analysts were skeptical of Lululemon (LULU), calling it a niche brand for yoga enthusiasts. But young consumers knew better. They understood that the brand was becoming a status symbol, driving high margins. The clothing became ubiquitous—a fashion statement adopted by high schoolers and college students nationwide. Those who invested early based on that immediate consumer observation saw massive returns.

The same applies today. Which brands are dominating the halls of your school? Are they sustainable companies? Are they using technology effectively? Are they constantly sold out? These aren't random events; they are key indicators of demand that translates directly into high stock prices.

STREAMING AND THE ATTENTION ECONOMY

THE BATTLE FOR YOUR ATTENTION IS THE BIGGEST GAME IN MEDIA, and it's fought by the biggest companies in the world: Disney (DIS), Netflix (NFLX), Amazon (AMZN), and others.

If you observe that everyone you know is canceling a major streaming service because the content is stale, or if they are all signing up for a new, niche platform that is crushing the competition, that is crucial investment data.

In the late 2010s, many teens migrated their entertainment consumption entirely away from cable television and straight to platforms like Netflix and YouTube. Wall Street eventually caught up, but the people who lived through that shift—the consumers—had the clearest view of the magnitude of that change.

THE GOLDEN RULE OF CONSUMER INVESTING

Use your experience to identify the companies that solve modern problems better than their competition. Ask yourself:

1. Which apps do I open daily and absolutely rely on? (Could be Microsoft, Google, or a smaller software company.)
2. Which products are so well-designed that people are willing to pay a premium for them? (Think Apple or specific high-end sneaker companies.)
3. Which services make my life easier or more entertaining, and appear to have no viable replacement? (These often include cloud storage, payment processors, or logistical giants.)

When you identify a company that successfully dominates a habit in your daily life, you have found a potential long-term winner. The next step, which we dive into in the following section, is applying simple valuation metrics to confirm whether the company's price matches its evident power.

You don't need to be a finance expert to spot a successful product; you just need to be a successful consumer. Your homework isn't a textbook; it's your daily life. Start paying attention to who is collecting the money every time you click, stream, or buy.

—★–★–★—

THE 30-SECOND VALUATION TEST: INSTANTLY KNOWING IF A STOCK IS 'ON SALE' OR HUGELY OVERPRICED

You've learned how to identify companies that are successful—companies that make products you love and that have a competitive edge. That's step one.

Step two, the one that separates the smart investors from the suckers, is figuring out if that company's stock is actually worth the price tag right now. You wouldn't pay $500 for a gaming console that costs $200 everywhere else, right? Yet, this happens every day in the stock market. People overpay for great companies simply because they are popular.

To avoid this, you need the single most important tool in basic stock analysis: the Price-to-Earnings Ratio, or P/E.

What is the P/E Ratio?

The P/E ratio is your 30-second valuation test. It tells you exactly how much investors are willing to pay for every dollar of annual profit a company generates. It's calculated simply:

P/E Ratio = Stock Price / Earnings Per Share (EPS)

Think of it this way: The P/E ratio is asking, "How many years of this company's current profit am I paying for right now?"

If a company's stock is trading at $100 per share, and it made $5 in profit (earnings) per share over the last year, the P/E ratio is 20 ($100 / $5 = 20).

This means you are essentially paying 20 years of current profit for that single share.

The instant litmus test is simple: The lower the P/E number, the cheaper the stock is relative to its current profits. The higher the P/E number, the more expensive it is relative to its current profits.

WHEN A STOCK IS HUGELY OVERPRICED (HIGH P/E)

If you see a stock with a P/E ratio of 50, 80, or even 100, you are looking at a very expensive stock. But why would anyone pay 100 times the company's annual profit?

The answer is Future Hope.

Companies with high P/E ratios are usually hyper-growth stocks (like certain high-flying tech or biotech firms). The market isn't paying for what the company did last year; they are betting heavily on what the company will do five or ten years from now. They expect profits to double or triple very quickly, making that 100 P/E seem like 30 P/E in retrospect.

This is where the risk is highest. If the company fails to deliver that explosive growth, the stock price crashes immediately because the valuation was based purely on extreme optimism.

Example: If a hot new AI company has a P/E of 90, it means investors are paying an enormous "hype tax" based on the assumption that AI will take over the world.

When a Stock is 'On Sale' (Low P/E)

If you find a solid, stable company with a P/E ratio under 15 (sometimes even under 10), this suggests the stock is trading cheaply relative to its current cash flow. These are often called "value stocks."

These companies are usually mature, established businesses—big banks, utility companies, or large manufacturing firms. They aren't expected to grow 50% year over year, but they are reliable profit generators. When you buy a low P/E stock, you are buying a lot of real, proven profit for a relatively low price.

This offers a margin of safety. If the company is trading at 10 times earnings (P/E of 10), even if the market gets volatile, the price is less likely to collapse because the underlying profits are real and consistent.

Using P/E Correctly: Context is King

While the P/E ratio is the ultimate 30-second test, you must use it with context. You can't compare a utility company (stable, low growth) with a P/E of 12 to a streaming company (high growth, high expansion costs) with a P/E of 60 and conclude the streaming company is "overpriced." They operate in different worlds with different expectations.

To use the P/E test effectively, compare:

1. The company's current P/E to its historical average P/E. Is it cheaper or more expensive than it usually is?

2. The company's P/E to the P/E of its direct competitors in the same industry. Is it cheaper than its direct rivals?

If you find a company you love that operates in a fast-growing industry, and its P/E ratio is significantly lower than its peers, congratulations—you may have found an asset that is currently "on sale." This quick metric helps you move past simply buying a brand name and forces you to focus on the cold, hard numbers of profitability.

—★-★-★—

IGNORING 99% OF FINANCIAL NEWS: THE 4 KEY MACRO-DRIVERS THAT ACTUALLY MOVE YOUR MONEY

You have just spent hours researching P/E ratios and understanding which companies are fundamentally sound. Now, you flip on the financial news to validate your choices, and immediately, chaos erupts.

A screaming pundit claims, "The market is collapsing! Sell everything!" Another host predicts a massive rally based on a tweet from an obscure CEO. The screen flashes red arrows, complex charts, and headlines that change every four minutes.

Here is your secret weapon: Ignore 99% of that noise.

If you are investing for the long term—which you absolutely must be as a young investor—then the daily, weekly, or even monthly swings of the market are distractions. They are gossip, not information. Trying to trade based on daily news is like trying to drive across the country by constantly looking in the rearview mirror.

Instead of chasing headlines, you need to understand the four giant, slow-moving levers that actually drive the market over the long term. These macro-drivers affect every single company, from Apple to the small regional bank, and they are the only news worth paying attention to a few times a year.

THE FOUR MACRO-DRIVERS THAT MATTER

WHEN YOU HEAR A FINANCIAL REPORT, ASK YOURSELF: IS THIS RElated to one of the four foundational forces listed below? If the answer is no, stop reading.

1. Interest Rates: The Price of Money

Think of the economy as a giant borrowing machine. Businesses borrow money to build new factories, hire new staff, and develop new products. Consumers borrow money to buy houses or cars.

Interest rates are the cost of that borrowing, and they are largely controlled by central banks, like the Federal Reserve (The Fed) in the U.S.

The Impact:

Low Interest Rates: Borrowing is cheap. Companies expand rapidly, which increases profits and usually pushes stock prices up. This is rocket fuel for the market.

High Interest Rates: Borrowing is expensive. Companies slow down expansion, which can shrink profits. Debt becomes harder to manage. This acts as a drag on the market, sometimes causing prices to fall.

When The Fed talks about raising or lowering rates, the entire market pays attention, because they are changing the gravitational pull of the economy.

2. Inflation: The Shrinking Power of Cash

Inflation is simply the rate at which the general cost of goods and services rises, and consequently, the purchasing power of your dollar falls. If inflation is 5%, that means a $10 movie ticket will cost $10.50 next year.

The Impact:

If you save cash under your mattress while inflation is 5%, you are losing 5% of your wealth every year. Inflation is the single greatest reason why saving money fails, and why investing is mandatory.

Investors react to inflation primarily because central banks react to it. If inflation runs too high, the central bank's automatic response is to raise interest rates (Driver 1) to cool down the economy. Inflation often dictates the cost of raw materials and labor, directly impacting company profit margins.

3. Technological & Social Development

While the first two drivers are economic, this third driver is about innovation—the single biggest long-term engine of wealth creation. This includes technological shifts (AI, biotech, space tech, blockchain) and fundamental social shifts (the transition to renewable energy, changing demographics, remote work).

The Impact:

These developments determine which companies win and which ones go extinct over the next decade. Did you invest in companies making CD players in 2005? Oops. Did you invest in streaming companies in 2010? Congratulations.

As a teen, this is your greatest advantage. You understand the emerging trends and consumer habits better than the 50-year-old analysts on Wall Street. Pay attention to what your generation is adopting, because those companies are the market leaders of tomorrow.

4. Global Economic Health and Stability

This driver encompasses the broad mood of the global economy: Are we in a strong period of growth, or are we facing a recession? Is there major geopolitical conflict (war, trade tariffs) or a global crisis (like a pandemic) that fundamentally changes supply chains and consumer behavior?

The Impact:

When economies are healthy, employment is high, people spend money, and corporate profits flourish. This creates a bull market (a rising market).

When stability is threatened (recessions, wars), confidence drops. Consumers pull back spending, and investors pull back risk. This causes bear markets (falling markets).

As a long-term investor, you ignore the daily fear, but you pay attention to fundamental shifts in economic strength. For instance, knowing if major economies (like the U.S. or China) are predicted to enter a recession allows you to anticipate broader corporate profit declines, but it should never prompt you to panic-sell your long-term, high-quality assets.

Focus on these four major currents. They tell you the story of the next five to ten years. Everything else is just commentary.

—★–★–★—

SHOCKING TRUTH: WHY CHECKING YOUR PORTFOLIO EVERY DAY GUARANTEES YOU'LL LOSE MONEY

When you launched your investment account, you might have felt a rush of adrenaline. It's exciting! Suddenly, that money you earned stacking shelves or walking dogs is working for you. It's natural to want to check your phone every few hours to see if Apple stock just bought you a new pair of headphones.

Stop. Put the phone down. Delete the app icon if you have to.

The shocking truth about successful investing—especially for young people—is that the more often you look at your portfolio, the higher the chances you'll make a stupid, emotional mistake and lose money. Checking your portfolio daily is the absolute quickest way to sabotage the biggest advantage you have: time.

This book is your playbook for becoming a multi-decade compounding champion. It is absolutely not a guide to day trading.

WHY DAILY MONITORING IS YOUR ENEMY

THINK OF YOUR INVESTMENTS LIKE PLANTING A SEED IN THE GARDEN. You know that seed is going to grow into a massive tree over twenty years. If you dig it up every single morning to see if the roots have extended 1/16th of an inch, you aren't helping it grow; you're killing it.

The stock market is powered by two things: long-term economic growth and short-term human emotion. When you check the price every hour, you are focusing solely on the short-term emotion—the noise.

The value of a fantastic company like Google doesn't actually change because some hedge fund sold a billion dollars worth of stock at 11:30 AM. But when you see that momentary dip reflected in your account, your brain doesn't register it as a temporary technical fluctuation. It screams, "LOSS! SELL NOW!"

This is called panic selling, and it is the single most destructive habit an investor can have. Investing is designed to reward patience; daily checking is designed to reward impatience.

DAY TRADING: THE SIREN SONG OF STRESS

IF YOU'VE HEARD STORIES OF PEOPLE MAKING THOUSANDS OF DOLLARS buying and selling stock ten times a day, you've heard of day trading. It sounds glamorous, but for 99% of people, especially beginners, it is an express lane to losing capital.

Day trading requires massive amounts of time, specialized software, deep market knowledge, and an iron will. It's a full-time job. It's gambling. Your goal, by contrast, is to leverage compounding interest so that your money is working while you're in class, playing video games, or sleeping.

Your strategy is 'Set It and Forget It' (mostly). Day trading's strategy is 'Stare at the Screen Until You Go Blind.' Stick to the strategy that actually makes you rich without ruining your life.

THE INEVITABLE DIP: OPPORTUNITY, NOT DISASTER

The market doesn't always go up. It will drop. It will crash. This is guaranteed. In your lifetime as an investor, you will see multiple recessions and financial crises.

When this happens—when the news is screaming about a "market meltdown" and your portfolio is down 20%—the temptation to pull all your money out will be immense. Your brain will tell you: "Get out before you lose it all!"

But remember this simple principle: A loss is only realized when you sell.

When the market dips, your quality index funds and strong individual companies don't suddenly become terrible businesses. They become discounted. They are now "on sale."

If you had planned to buy $100 worth of an S&P 500 fund every month, and the price drops by 15%, your $100 contribution now buys you 15% more shares. You are literally acquiring more assets for the same amount of money. This is how smart investors make fortunes. They don't panic; they buy low.

If you are checking your portfolio daily, you will feel the pain of that 20% drop too acutely, and you will sell, cementing your loss right before the recovery begins. If you check quarterly, you see the dip, you ride it out, and you keep buying cheaply.

Your job as a young investor is simple:

1. Invest regularly (Dollar-Cost Averaging).

2. Invest in quality assets (Index funds and great companies).

3. Do nothing else.

Limit yourself to checking your account once a month, or better yet, once a quarter. This disciplined patience is the hidden secret to long-term wealth that the daily stock chatter never reveals.

CHAPTER SIX

—★-★-★—

THE 7-DAY WEALTH LAUNCHPAD: BUILDING YOUR FIRST 'SET-IT-AND-FORGET-IT' PORTFOLIO (DAYS 1-3)

CONGRATULATIONS. YOU MADE IT. YOU HAVE THE MINDSET (Chapter 1), the money management skills (Chapter 2), the account setup (Chapter 3), and the knowledge of what assets exist (Chapter 4), plus a little bit of research savvy (Chapter 5).

Now it's time to move from theory to action. This is the moment where you stop reading about investing and start actually investing.

The next seven days are structured to take you through the entire process of building, executing, and automating your first portfolio. We are going to make decisions that will set the course for your financial future. This chapter covers Days 1 through 3—the planning and selection phase. By the time you finish this, you will know exactly what assets to buy and how much money to dedicate to each one.

Get ready to build the wealth machine.

DAY 1: THE 'SLEEP TEST' - DISCOVERING YOUR TRUE INVESTMENT APPETITE (WHY BEING YOUNG MEANS YOU CAN AFFORD TO BE RECKLESS)

Before you buy a single share, you need to understand your relationship with risk.

Most investment books treat risk like a four-letter word. They tell you to be safe, be conservative, and stick to boring assets. But guess what? Most investment books aren't written for 16-year-olds with an investment horizon spanning the next five decades.

Your single greatest financial superpower right now is time. Time is the great neutralizer of market volatility. If the stock market drops 20% next year, it hurts an adult who plans to retire in five years. But for you? It means everything is on sale, and you have 40 years for it to recover—and then some.

Therefore, your age allows you to be financially "reckless." This doesn't mean gambling your allowance on meme stocks; it means embracing higher volatility (and therefore, higher potential growth) because you have the time to withstand any short-term dips.

The "Sleep Test"

Your risk tolerance is simply the amount of market fluctuation you can endure without panicking and selling everything. We call this the Sleep Test: If the market drops 15% overnight, are you able to sleep soundly, knowing that historically, the market always recovers and then climbs higher? Or are you staring at the ceiling, ready to liquidate everything at a loss?

Take a moment to assess where you fall:

1. Conservative (Low Risk): You are putting money away for something critical in the next 1–3 years (e.g., a specific college payment, a high-cost item). You cannot afford major dips.

Strategy: Focus heavily on bonds, CDs, and very stable index funds. (Not recommended for most teen investors.)

2. Moderate (Medium Risk): You are willing to see your account drop 10-20% knowing it will recover, but major dips cause some stress.

Strategy: A healthy mix of broad index funds and a small allocation to individual growth stocks. (The sweet spot for many beginners.)

3. Aggressive (High Risk): You see a market crash as a buying opportunity. You are investing for decades, and short-term volatility doesn't scare you because your goal is maximum long-term growth.

Strategy: Heavily weighted in high-growth stock index funds and a larger portion dedicated to researched individual stocks. (Highly recommended for teen investors who are serious about wealth.)

The Default Setting for the Young Investor

Because you are playing the long game (the decades game), your default setting should be Moderate to Aggressive. You are optimizing for growth, not stability. Stability is for people who need the cash in the short term. You are accumulating assets that will have time to compound exponentially.

Day 1 is complete when you have honestly assessed your tolerance. We will build the portfolio based on an Aggressive Growth mandate: maximum exposure to the stock market, tempered by smart diversification.

Day 2: The 80% Safety Net: Selecting the 3 Tickers That Guaranteed Growth for Decades

Welcome to Day 2: The Foundation.

When you build a skyscraper, you don't start with the penthouse; you start with an unbreakable concrete foundation. In your portfolio, that foundation is made up of low-cost, broadly diversified index funds.

This section, representing 60% to 80% of your total investment capital, is the "Set-It-and-Forget-It" part of your portfolio. Your goal here is to purchase the global economy, ensuring that no matter which single company wins or loses, your overall portfolio still benefits.

The key to your safety net is that it must be invested in something that has historically averaged 8% to 10% annual returns over the last century—which is the entire stock market.

The Three Pillars of Your Core Portfolio

We are going to divide your core safety net into three simple, broad categories. You only need to pick one ticker from each category, and you're done.

Pillar 1: The US Market Titan (40-50% of Total Portfolio)

This is your stake in the 500 largest companies in the United States (the S&P 500). If Apple, Microsoft, Google, and Amazon are doing well, this investment does well. It's the most reliable engine of wealth creation in history.

Key Tickers to Search (Look for the lowest expense ratio):

VOO (Vanguard S&P 500 ETF)

IVV (iShares Core S&P 500 ETF)

FXAIX (Fidelity 500 Index Fund)

Pillar 2: The Total Market Sweep (10-20% of Total Portfolio)

While the S&P 500 is great, it misses smaller, potentially faster-growing companies. The Total US Stock Market fund includes the S&P 500 plus thousands of mid-size and smaller companies, giving you full coverage of the US economy.

Key Tickers to Search:

VTI (Vanguard Total Stock Market ETF)

ITOT (iShares Core Total US Stock Market ETF)

Pillar 3: The International Player (10-20% of Total Portfolio)

The world is a big place, and sometimes the best growth happens overseas (in Japan, Germany, emerging markets, etc.). Putting a slice of your money here ensures that if the US market is having a bad decade, your international investments can pick up the slack. This is crucial diversification.

Key Tickers to Search:

VXUS (Vanguard Total International Stock ETF)

IXUS (iShares Core MSCI Total International Stock ETF)

Why 80% Goes Here

This foundation guarantees you participate in the historical, compounding growth of the market while minimizing the effort required on your part. You never have to research these stocks; you just have to trust that the global economy will continue to grow over the next 40 years. If you believe that human ingenuity and capitalism will continue, then this 80% is guaranteed to grow.

Day 3: The Profit Punch: How to Identify 2 High-Growth 'Strikers' to Boost Your Returns by 25%

Now for the fun part. After securing your 60-80% foundation, you have 20% to 40% of your capital remaining. We are calling these your "Strikers."

In a soccer game, the defenders and goalie are your S&P 500—they are reliable and prevent catastrophic loss. But the strikers—they are the ones who score the goals.

The goal of this portion is not safety; it's outperformance. You are aiming to identify the next Apple or Tesla before they become household names, or at least identify the companies that you believe will dominate their sector for the next decade.

This is where you apply the research methods from Chapter 5.

The Striker Strategy Blueprint (20-40% Allocation)

Limit yourself to purchasing 3 to 5 individual stocks or niche, high-growth ETFs in this portion. Anything more than five becomes too complex to track, and you lose the concentration needed for massive gains.

Step 1: Focus on What You Know (The Consumer Advantage)

Remember Chapter 5? Use your perspective as a savvy consumer.

Are you obsessed with a new direct-to-consumer brand, gaming company, or social platform that has exploded in the last year?

Is there a company whose product is so good that you cannot imagine a competitor stealing their market share in the next five years? (Think software, streaming, chip manufacturing.)

Is there an industry that is clearly the future (AI, space, genomics) and you know a strong leader in that space?

Step 2: Apply the 30-Second Valuation Test (The P/E Check)

Before buying, quickly check the company's Price-to-Earnings (P/E) ratio.

If the P/E is extremely low (under 10), it might signal a deeply undervalued company, or it might signal a dying one. Proceed with caution.

If the P/E is very high (over 50), it means investors are pricing in massive future growth. Buying these stocks is risky because if the growth slows down even a little, the stock price can crash.

Look for strong, growing companies with reasonable P/E ratios (15 to 30) that show steady revenue and profit increases.

Step 3: Define Your Holding Thesis

Do not buy a stock just because someone on the internet told you to. You must write down (even mentally) why you own it. This is your Holding Thesis.

Example Thesis for a Gaming Company (GME): "I own this stock because I believe their CEO has a revolutionary plan to pivot the company into a blockchain-integrated metaverse gaming platform that will dominate the industry by 2030."

If your thesis breaks (e.g., the CEO quits, the plan fails), then you sell. If the stock drops 20% but your thesis is still solid, you hold—or even buy more.

This 20-40% portion allows you to take calculated risks that could significantly boost your total returns, giving you an edge over investors who only stick to index funds. Day 3 is about selecting these potential home runs.

The Iron Shield: How to Protect Your Portfolio So One Bad Stock Can Never Wipe You Out

Congratulations! You have identified the players for your team: the rock-solid defense (index funds) and the high-powered offense (individual stocks). Now, we need to finalize the allocation to create the Iron Shield—diversification.

Diversification is the insurance policy of investing. It simply means ensuring that no single event, asset, or company can ruin your entire financial future. You achieve diversification by splitting your money across different sectors, company sizes, and geographies.

The Starter Portfolio Allocation Template

Since you are young and aggressive, here is a highly effective, low-maintenance template designed for maximum growth and minimal maintenance:

The 70/30 Aggressive Growth Starter Portfolio

Portfolio Slice	Allocation	Purpose	Examples (Tickers)
Broad Market Core	70%	Safety & Guaranteed Growth	VOO, VTI, VXUS (Split among the three)
Individual Strikers	30%	High-Growth Potential	3-5 individual stocks (e.g., tech, clean energy, gaming)

Why does this allocation work so well?

1. The Weight of Reliability: Even if two of your individual stocks go bankrupt (and yes, they might), you only lose a small fraction of your total capital. The 70% invested in the broad market will absorb the shock and continue to compound, meaning your overall portfolio health remains strong.

2. Emotional Control: If the market drops, you know the biggest chunk of your money is secure in low-cost, resilient index funds. This prevents the panicked selling that costs amateur investors fortunes.

3. Maximum Time Leverage: By dedicating 70% to growth assets (all stocks, no bonds yet), you maximize the potential for compounding over decades.

The Final Protection Step: Dollar-Cost Averaging

We will cover the execution in Chapter 7, but the final component of the Iron Shield is deciding to invest regularly. When you invest a set amount of money at regular intervals (say, $50 every paycheck), you are practicing Dollar-Cost Averaging (DCA).

DCA is an Iron Shield because it protects you from the emotional mistake of trying to "time the market." You don't have to guess if tomorrow's price will be lower or higher. You buy regardless. If the price is low, you get more shares. If the price is high, you get fewer. Over the long run, this disciplined, automated approach consistently outperforms those who try to guess the dips and peaks.

You now have a complete, researched, and risk-assessed plan. Days 1, 2, and 3 are finished. You know where your money is coming from and exactly where it's going. In the next chapter, we execute the plan by setting up the automation and placing those first crucial trades.

—★—★—★—

DAY 1: THE 'SLEEP TEST' - DISCOVERING YOUR TRUE INVESTMENT APPETITE (WHY BEING YOUNG MEANS YOU CAN AFFORD TO BE RECKLESS)

THE SINGLE MOST CRITICAL STEP YOU CAN TAKE BEFORE PUTTING A dollar into the market is determining your "risk tolerance." This sounds complicated, but it's actually a very simple question: How much volatility (swings up and down) can you handle before you panic and sell everything?

The ultimate barometer for this is the "Sleep Test." If you invest $100 into a stock and that stock drops to $70 overnight, are you going to lose sleep, or are you going to shrug and check the price again next week? Your answer dictates your entire strategy.

Why are we focusing on this first? Because your age is the greatest financial tool you will ever possess.

The Teenager's Ultimate Advantage: The Freedom to Be Reckless

When a 45-year-old invests, they might be planning for retirement in 20 years. If the market crashes 50%, that's a catastrophe. They have limited time to recover, and they often need that money relatively soon.

You? You are playing a 50-year game.

If the market crashes 50% tomorrow, you have decades to not just recover, but to profit massively from the recovery. Every time the market goes down, it's not a loss; it's a giant clearance sale on the best companies in the world. An older investor might panic and sell; you have the luxury of buying more.

This time advantage is why financial advisors universally recommend that younger investors maintain a high-growth, high-risk portfolio. You should prioritize the potential for massive returns over short-term stability, because time guarantees stability in the long run.

In short: you are practically immune to short-term market fluctuations. You can afford to be "reckless" in the pursuit of maximum growth.

Ready to find your level? Grab a pen or open a note app and answer the following questions. Tally up your points at the end.

THE INVESTMENT APPETITE QUIZ

For each question, choose the statement that best represents your true feelings, not what you think you should feel.

QUESTION 1: WHAT IS THE PRIMARY TIMELINE FOR THE MONEY YOU ARE INVESTING?

A. I might need this money in 2 to 5 years (e.g., for college tuition, a big trip, or a car). (1 Point)

B. I don't need this money for 5 to 10 years, but I'd like to see it grow steadily. (2 Points)

C. I don't need this money for 15+ years; this is purely for long-term wealth building and financial freedom. (3 Points)

QUESTION 2: IMAGINE YOU INVEST $500. NEXT MONTH, THE STOCK MARKET DIPS, AND YOUR ACCOUNT VALUE DROPS TO $400 (A 20% LOSS). HOW DO YOU REACT?

A. I would feel worried, pull the remaining $400 out, and wait for things to stabilize before trying again. (1 Point)

B. I would feel frustrated, but I would leave the money alone and continue making my regular monthly contributions. (2 Points)

C. I would feel excited because everything is on sale. I would try to find extra cash to double my next investment contribution. (3 Points)

QUESTION 3: WHICH INVESTMENT OUTCOME IS MORE APPEALING TO YOU?

A. An investment that almost certainly earns 4% per year, every year, but never drops in value. (1 Point)

B. An investment that might earn 12% in a good year and lose 5% in a bad year, averaging 8% over time. (2 Points)

C. An investment that could potentially earn 20% in a good year, but might also lose 20% in a bad year, averaging 10% over time. (3 Points)

QUESTION 4: HOW MUCH ATTENTION DO YOU PLAN TO PAY TO YOUR PORTFOLIO?

A. I want to check my account statement daily to make sure I'm not losing money. (1 Point)

B. I will check my portfolio once a month to ensure I am still contributing regularly. (2 Points)

C. I plan to set up automatic contributions and ignore the account for 6 to 12

TALLYING YOUR RESULTS: YOUR RISK PROFILE

CALCULATE YOUR TOTAL POINTS AND SEE WHERE YOU LAND.

4-5 POINTS: THE CONSERVATIVE INVESTOR (SAFETY FIRST)

Your priority is capital preservation—not losing money. While this mindset is smart for short-term goals, it is typically too cautious for long-term investing when you are young.

Your strategy should heavily favor the core safety assets we discuss on Day 2: ultra-safe index funds, bonds, and Certificates of Deposit (CDs). You should put 90%+ of your money into broad funds to ensure maximum stability, even if it means slower growth. You are willing to sacrifice potential returns for peace of mind.

6-8 POINTS: THE MODERATE INVESTOR (BALANCED GROWTH)

This is a healthy and common approach. You are willing to accept some short-term dips in exchange for solid, long-term growth. You recognize that losses are part of the game but you aren't actively seeking out the highest-risk assets.

Your ideal strategy (which we will build on Day 2 and Day 3) is a balanced approach: roughly 70% in broad, reliable index funds, and 30% dedicated to higher-growth individual stocks or sector-specific funds (like technology).

9-12 POINTS: THE AGGRESSIVE INVESTOR (GROWTH MAXIMIZER)

CONGRATULATIONS! YOUR RISK TOLERANCE IS PERFECTLY ALIGNED with your time horizon. You understand that in the long run, market dips are opportunities, not disasters. You are focused entirely on maximizing total return, even if it means experiencing significant volatility along the way.

Your strategy should be dominated by high-growth vehicles: 60-80% in reliable index funds, and the remainder dedicated to individual growth stocks and aggressive, niche ETFs. You are positioned to capture the highest potential returns the market offers, leveraging your decades-long runway to ride out any storms.

The Key Takeaway: The vast majority of investors under the age of 25 should be pursuing a Moderate or Aggressive strategy. If your score was Conservative, that is totally fine—your "Sleep Test" is the most important measure—but you should challenge yourself to follow the Moderate strategy plan first. Remember: you have time to recover from virtually any mistake, but you can never recover the returns you missed out on by being too afraid to start.

DAY 2: THE 80% SAFETY NET: SELECTING THE 3 TICKERS THAT GUARANTEED GROWTH FOR DECADES

YESTERDAY, YOU DECIDED HOW MUCH RISK YOU COULD HANDLE (A lot, since you're young). Today, we're implementing the most crucial principle of long-term wealth: building a bedrock of incredibly solid, boring investments that promise growth over decades.

Think of your portfolio as a superhero team. You need a powerhouse core—the dependable foundation that always shows up and never quits. That core is your 80% Safety Net, and it is made up exclusively of broad, low-cost index funds.

The goal here is not to beat the market; the goal is to own the market.

Why 60% to 80%?

If you were a betting person, would you bet on one single athlete to win every single race for the next 40 years? Or would you bet on the entire league?

By dedicating the majority of your capital to broad index funds, you are betting on the long-term success of the entire global economy—the collective genius of thousands of companies. This is the single highest-probability bet in finance. It's what legendary investor Warren Buffett recommends for almost everyone.

What exactly are we buying? We are buying two things: the US market and the International market.

THE MAGIC OF THE INDEX FUND

An index fund (often packaged as an ETF, or Exchange-Traded Fund) is a basket of investments designed to mirror the performance of a specific market index. The most famous index is the S&P 500, which holds 500 of the largest, most successful companies in the US (Apple, Microsoft, Google, etc.).

When you buy a single share of an S&P 500 ETF, you are instantly invested in all 500 companies. If Apple has a bad quarter, Netflix or Amazon might pick up the slack, cushioning any loss. This is immediate, powerful diversification, and it's why index funds are the foundation of any smart portfolio.

The other massive advantage is the cost, measured by the expense ratio. This is the tiny annual fee they charge to manage the fund. The index funds listed below have expense ratios so low (often 0.03%), you will barely notice them. They are essentially free.

THE THREE TICKERS THAT GUARANTEED GROWTH FOR DECADES

YOUR MISSION FOR DAY 2 IS TO RESEARCH AND SELECT THREE TICKers that will make up the majority of your investment portfolio. These are the workhorses that require zero attention, but deliver reliable 8-10% average annual returns over the long run.

CATEGORY 1: THE US TOTAL STOCK MARKET (YOUR PRIMARY ENGINE)

THIS TICKER GIVES YOU INSTANT OWNERSHIP OF VIRTUALLY EVERY publicly traded US company, big and small. It ensures you capture all the growth the American economy offers. This should make up the largest portion of your safety net (e.g., 50% of your total capital).

TICKER OPTION 1: VTI (VANGUARD TOTAL STOCK MARKET ETF)

WHY IT'S GREAT: EXTREMELY LOW EXPENSE RATIO (NEARLY FREE) AND holds over 3,500 different stocks. When someone says they are "invested in the market," this is often what they mean.

TICKER OPTION 2: VOO (VANGUARD S&P 500 ETF)

WHY IT'S GREAT: THIS FOCUSES PURELY ON THE 500 BIGGEST COMPAnies, which are generally the most stable. Historically, the S&P 500 has been the greatest wealth generator in the world.

Action Step: In your brokerage app, search for either VTI or VOO. Look at its history. Notice how it always recovers from dips and trends upward over time.

CATEGORY 2: THE INTERNATIONAL MARKET (THE GLOBAL DIVERSIFIER)

A COMMON MISTAKE NEW INVESTORS MAKE IS PUTTING 100% OF their money into the US market. While the US is powerful, true diversification means owning assets outside the US borders as well. Sometimes foreign economies outperform the US, and sometimes they lag, but by owning both, you ensure your portfolio never misses out.

This ticker should make up about 20-30% of your total capital.

TICKER OPTION 3: VXUS (VANGUARD TOTAL INTERNATIONAL STOCK ETF)

WHY IT'S GREAT: THIS FUND HOLDS THOUSANDS OF STOCKS ACROSS developed and emerging foreign markets, but excludes the US. It is the perfect counterbalance to VTI or VOO. It ensures that if the US economy hits a rough patch, your money invested in Europe, Asia, and other global regions can stabilize your returns.

YOUR DAY 2 ACTION PLAN: THE 80% ALLOCATION

ASSUMING YOU HAVE $500 READY TO INVEST (OR WHATEVER YOUR initial capital is), here is how Day 2 breaks down:

1. Commit to the 80%: Determine 80% of your capital (e.g., $400 of $500). This money is only going into index funds.

2. Split the Global Pie: Divide that 80% between the US and International. A good starting point is a 70/30 split within that bucket.

Sample Portfolio Breakdown (If your total starting capital is $500):

Safety Net (80% Total: $400)

4. US Market (70% of Safety Net): $280 invested in VTI or VOO

5. International Market (30% of Safety Net): $120 invested in VXUS

The remaining 20% ($100) is your "Profit Punch" money, which we will dedicate to individual, high-growth stocks tomorrow on Day 3.

Remember: This 80% chunk is your set-it-and-forget-it money. It's what will grow reliably while you finish high school, go to college, and start your career. Do not check it daily. Do not worry about it during market dips. It is the boring, powerful engine driving your long-term wealth.

—★-★-★—

DAY 3: THE PROFIT PUNCH: HOW TO IDENTIFY 2 HIGH-GROWTH 'STRIKERS' TO BOOST YOUR RETURNS BY 25%

Welcome to Day 3. If Day 2 was about building the massive, unshakable foundation of your financial life, Day 3 is about giving that foundation rocket fuel.

Yesterday, you allocated 60% to 80% of your initial capital into broad, diversified index funds—your defensive line, your goalies, and your reliable midfield. They are the stable core that guarantees participation in the long-term growth of the global economy.

Today, we are looking for your Strikers.

The 20% to 40% portion of your portfolio is where you allocate capital to individual stocks that you believe have explosive, game-changing potential. This is the portion designed to significantly boost your overall returns beyond the market average, potentially adding 25% or more to your long-term wealth—but it comes with a higher risk profile.

The goal here is not to pick ten stocks. The goal is to pick two or three companies that you genuinely believe will dominate their respective industries for the next decade.

The single most important rule when selecting your Strikers is the 10-Year Test.

THE 10-YEAR TEST: THE ONLY FILTER YOU NEED

BEFORE YOU CLICK 'BUY' ON ANY INDIVIDUAL STOCK, LOOK AT THE company's services and ask yourself: "Do I believe this company will be substantially bigger, more powerful, and more successful in 2035 than it is today?"

If the answer is anything less than an absolute, confident "Yes," then it's not a striker for your portfolio. It's a gamble, and we don't gamble with our future.

Why 10 years? Because the market is noisy. Every single day, analysts will scream about a new quarterly report, interest rate hikes, or global politics. All of that noise is irrelevant to you. When you invest as a teenager, you are playing the long game. You can afford to ignore the daily drama because your strategy is based on fundamental change, not short-term trading.

This long-term focus immediately eliminates most short-lived trends, meme stocks, and companies that rely on a single passing fad (like a specific viral app that might be forgotten in two years).

HOW TO TURN YOUR PERSPECTIVE INTO PROFIT

THIS IS WHERE YOU LEVERAGE THE RESEARCH SKILLS WE DRILLED IN Chapter 5. You have a massive advantage over 60-year-old hedge fund managers: you are the consumer of tomorrow. You know what products are genuinely sticky, what technology is changing everything, and what companies are innovating.

Here are the three steps to selecting your high-growth Strikers:

1. Identify Your Conviction Areas (The Consumer Insight)

Think about the products, services, and companies you interact with every week that genuinely impress you and your peers.

Are you constantly using a specific piece of software for school or gaming? Are you reliant on a particular brand of athletic gear that seems to be everywhere? Is there a niche streaming service that is out-innovating the big players?

Write down 5 to 10 companies that meet the following criteria:

A. They solve a real problem (or provide compelling entertainment/service).

B. They have a loyal, growing customer base (your friends are using it).

C. They feel necessary, not just nice-to-have.

For instance, 10 years ago, a young investor might have looked at a company like Netflix and realized: "Everyone is cutting cable; this subscription model is the future." That insight, based on personal experience, would have been gold. Now, look for the next Netflix.

2. Run the P/E Valuation Test (Is It On Sale?)

Once you have a shortlist of companies you believe in, you need to apply the 30-Second Valuation Test (Chapter 5) to make sure you aren't buying the stock when it is ridiculously overpriced.

A growth stock will almost always look "expensive" compared to a utility company because investors are paying for future growth. But there is a difference between expensive and insane.

If a company is growing its revenue and its potential market size aggressively, a P/E ratio above 30 might be justified. However, if a company that makes shoes has a P/E ratio of 80, it suggests the market is wildly optimistic, and a slight hiccup in performance could cause the stock to plummet.

Filter your list by checking the P/E ratio (easily accessible on any brokerage page or finance website). If the P/E is zero or negative, the company isn't profitable yet. That's a serious risk, but it's okay if you truly believe their product is revolutionizing the world (like Amazon was in its early days). Just understand that profitability is essential eventually.

3. Align With Macro Trends (Catching the Wave)

Individual stocks succeed when the entire industry is growing. This is called 'catching the macro wave.'

Your Strikers should ideally operate in fields that are guaranteed to see explosive growth over the next decade, regardless of who wins the political race next year. Look for exposure to these megatrends:

Artificial Intelligence (AI): Companies that build the chips, the software models, or the foundational infrastructure for AI.

The Digitization of Everything: Companies that transition physical industries (like finance, healthcare, or logistics) into purely digital, efficient platforms.

Clean Energy Transition: Manufacturers of batteries, infrastructure providers, or companies dedicated to reducing carbon footprints.

Next-Gen Gaming/Metaverse: Platforms and hardware providers for immersive digital experiences.

When you invest in a company riding one of these massive waves, you benefit not just from that company's success, but from the tailwind of global progress.

THE STRIKER ALLOCATION STRATEGY

For your starting portfolio, dedicate no more than 40% of your money to these high-conviction individual stocks.

If you are just starting with $500, that means $100 to $200 should go toward 2-4 individual Strikers. Keep the number small so you can monitor them and understand their business model thoroughly.

Example Allocation (Aggressive Teen Strategy):

70% Index Funds (S&P 500/Total Market ETF)

30% Individual Stocks (3 companies you genuinely believe will thrive in 10+ years)

Why only 30%? Because if one of those individual stocks fails (which happens all the time, even to the best investors), the 70% foundation will cushion the blow. You will still participate in the general market upside, minimizing the impact of your inevitable mistakes.

This structure allows you to take calculated risks without jeopardizing your long-term goals. Your Strikers are your chance for exponential gains, but your Index Funds are your guarantee that you stay in the game.

THE IRON SHIELD: HOW TO PROTECT YOUR PORTFOLIO SO ONE BAD STOCK CAN NEVER WIPE YOU OUT

If the market were a game, diversification would be the cheat code for invincibility.

You've spent days identifying the cash you can invest, setting up the right account, and pinpointing companies you think will thrive. You have your core index funds and your individual "strikers." But what happens if one of those strikers gets hit by a scandal, a catastrophic product failure, or simply goes bankrupt?

If 100% of your capital was tied up in that one stock, you'd be wiped out. Game over.

This is the catastrophic risk that diversification—the Iron Shield—is designed to prevent.

The ancient wisdom is still the best: Never put all your eggs in one basket. If the basket tips, all the eggs break. In investing terms, if you put all your money into a single stock (say, a hot new gaming company), and that company releases a flop or gets bought out for pennies, your portfolio has no safety net.

Diversification is the act of spreading your investment eggs across so many different baskets (companies, industries, and asset types) that if one basket tips, the loss is merely an inconvenience, not an extinction-level event. Since you are still young and have decades for your money to grow, your diversification strategy can be simple and highly effective.

The goal of your Iron Shield is two-fold:

1. Guarantee you capture the returns of the entire global economy (the safe, boring money).

2. Limit the damage one bad decision can inflict on your entire financial future.

THE CORE & SATELLITE APPROACH

For beginning investors, we recommend the Core & Satellite approach, a simple template that dictates exactly where your money goes.

Your portfolio is divided into two distinct parts:

1. THE CORE (The Iron Shield): 70% to 80% of your total invested capital.

2. THE SATELLITE (The Profit Punch): 20% to 30% of your total invested capital.

Let's break down how this protects you:

Allocation for Safety (The Core: 70% - 80%)

This is where the majority of your money goes, and it is reserved exclusively for low-cost, broad-market index funds or ETFs (Exchange-Traded Funds).

Why so much here? Because these funds are already diversified for you. An S&P 500 fund, for example, is one single ticker that holds small pieces of 500 different American companies across every sector—tech, healthcare, finance, consumer goods, etc. If one company fails, 499 others are there to keep the fund afloat.

The 70-80% dedicated to the Core serves as your Iron Shield. This money is designed to track the general growth of the economy. It is stable, predictable (over the long term), and most importantly, it minimizes your initial risk exposure. You are betting on the market as a whole, which has always gone up eventually.

Allocation for Growth (The Satellite: 20% - 30%)

This smaller portion is dedicated to the higher-risk, higher-reward assets: your individual stocks. These are the 2-5 companies you researched thoroughly, the ones you believe have 5x or 10x growth potential.

This is the fun money, the aggressive money, but it is kept intentionally small. If your Netflix stock pick doubles in a year, you get a great boost to your overall return. But if that stock gets absolutely obliterated and drops 90%, it only affects a tiny fraction of your portfolio.

Let's run the math on worst-case protection:

Imagine you invested $1,000.

$700 (70%) went into a diversified S&P 500 Index Fund.

$300 (30%) was split evenly across three individual stocks (A, B, C) at $100 each.

Scenario: Stock A (a high-growth striker) goes bankrupt and loses 100% of its value.

Loss: $100.

Total Portfolio Value: $1,000 - $100 = $900.

Total Portfolio Loss: Only 10%.

The Iron Shield held strong. Even though one of your picks vanished completely, 90% of your capital remains intact and is still positioned to benefit from the market's long-term upward trajectory.

If, instead, you had been foolish enough to put $1,000 into only Stock A, your portfolio would be zero.

The Iron Shield ensures that no matter how smart you think your stock pick is, you are never betting your entire future on it. This allocation template is the simplest, most effective way to combine the reliable safety of index investing with the exciting potential of individual company research.

CHAPTER SEVEN

—★-★-★—

AUTOMATION & EXECUTION: MAKING YOUR MONEY MOVE WITHOUT YOU LIFTING A FINGER (DAYS 4-7)

We've spent the first few days of this program building the perfect theoretical portfolio, identifying low-cost ETFs, and selecting a few killer individual stocks. Now it's time for the execution phase—the moment you actually hand over your cash and start owning a piece of the future. This is where the rubber meets the road, and luckily, modern brokerage technology has made this process incredibly easy, removing the confusing paperwork and complex systems of the past.

The goal for the next four days (Days 4 through 7) is threefold: First, make the initial purchase efficiently and cheaply. Second, automate the entire system so you never have to think about it again. Third, build the mental discipline required to survive market chaos.

DAY 4: THE FRACTIONAL SHARE POWER-UP: HOW TO BUY GOOGLE STOCK EVEN IF YOU ONLY HAVE $10

In the old days, if you wanted to buy stock in a major company—say, Google (Alphabet) or Amazon—you were out of luck unless you had hundreds, sometimes thousands, of dollars just to purchase a single share. This created a massive barrier for young investors.

Enter: The Fractional Share Power-Up.

Most modern, teen-friendly brokerages (the ones we discussed in Chapter 3) now offer fractional shares. This means you don't have to buy a full share; you can buy a fraction of one, based on the dollar amount you specify.

For example, if one share of Amazon is $150, but you only have $50 allocated for that stock, you can instruct your brokerage to buy $50 worth of Amazon. They will simply give you 0.333 shares. You are now officially an owner, without needing a massive cash reserve. This is the feature that makes diversification possible even if you're starting with just $100.

PLACING YOUR FIRST ORDER: MARKET VS. LIMIT

WHEN YOU GO TO HIT THE "BUY" BUTTON, YOU'LL BE ASKED TO SElect your "Order Type." Don't worry; this isn't complex calculus. There are two main types you need to know:

1. Market Order: This is the most common and simplest choice. You are telling the brokerage, "Buy this stock or ETF right now at whatever the current market price is." Since prices fluctuate constantly, you might pay slightly more or slightly less than the price you saw 30 seconds ago, but for broad funds and long-term investments, the difference is negligible.

When to use it: Almost always. Use it for your large index fund purchases (the 80% safety net) and generally for individual stocks you are comfortable holding for years.

2. Limit Order: This is where you set a price ceiling. You are telling the brokerage, "I want to buy 10 shares of this stock, but only if the price drops to $X or lower." The order will wait until the stock hits that price, and if it never does, the order expires without filling.

When to use it: When buying individual stocks and you feel the current price is slightly too high, or if you are trying to take advantage of a market dip. For beginners, however, stick to Market Orders to keep things simple and ensure your capital gets invested immediately.

Step-by-Step Execution Checklist (Day 4)

1. Log into your brokerage account (which should be fully funded).

2. Search for the ticker symbol of your chosen core ETF (e.g., VOO or IVV).

3. Select "Trade" or "Buy."

4. Select "Market Order."

5. Instead of entering the number of shares, switch the input to "Dollar Amount."

6. Enter 60-80% of your total capital (as planned in Day 2).

7. Click "Review Order" and then "Submit."

8. Repeat the process for your international ETF (if applicable).

9. Repeat the process for your 2-3 high-growth individual stocks (the Profit Punch from Day 3), allocating the remaining capital using fractional shares.

Congratulations. You have executed your first trades. You are now officially an owner.

THE DOLLAR-COST AVERAGING MACHINE™: YOUR AUTO-PILOT STRATEGY THAT DEFEATS MARKET ANXIETY

If Day 4 was about the initial launch, Days 5 and 6 are about building the autopilot system.

Imagine you are trying to hit a moving target in the dark. That's what it feels like when people try to "time the market"—they try to buy stocks only when they are at their lowest price. This is impossible. Even professional investors with teams of analysts cannot predict the market's bottom with any consistency.

The alternative, and the gold standard for long-term investors, is Dollar-Cost Averaging (DCA).

DCA is simple: Instead of trying to dump a huge chunk of money into the market all at once, you invest a fixed amount of money at regular intervals, regardless of whether the market is high or low.

Why DCA is the Ultimate Hack for Teen Investors

1. It Removes Emotion: You eliminate the guesswork and anxiety that comes with deciding when to invest. If you get paid on the 15th and 30th of the month, your money gets invested on the 16th and 1st. No analysis required.

2. It Forces Discipline: You are automatically obeying the "Pay Yourself First" rule (Chapter 2). If the money is moved automatically to your brokerage, you can't spend it on frivolous things.

3. It Buys More When Prices Are Low: This is the genius of DCA. When the market is high, your $100 buys fewer shares. When the market dips (which it always does sometimes), your same $100 buys more shares. Over time, this keeps your average cost low, which increases your overall return significantly.

Building Your DCA Machine (Days 5 & 6)

The process involves setting up two automatic transfers:

Step 1: Auto-Deposit

Set up a recurring transfer from your checking or savings account (the one where your allowance or job money lands) directly into your brokerage account.

Frequency: Align this with your cash flow. If you get paid every two weeks, set up a bi-weekly deposit.

Amount: Set this to the disposable investment amount you calculated in Chapter 2. Start small if you need to, but be consistent. Even $50 every two weeks adds up to $1,300 a year—and that money is immediately compounding.

Step 2: Auto-Invest

This step takes place entirely within the brokerage platform. You tell the brokerage which assets to buy automatically with the cash that arrives.

Set up recurring buys for your core ETFs (e.g., $40 of VOO every time the money lands).

Set up recurring buys for your individual stocks, utilizing the fractional share feature (e.g., $10 of Tesla every time the money lands).

Once these two systems are locked in, your work is essentially done. You have built a perpetual wealth machine that feeds itself. You're no longer trading; you are simply accumulating ownership in the world's best companies, automatically, perpetually, and without the anxiety of trying to guess the next market move.

——★–★–★——

THE QUARTERLY PORTFOLIO CHECK-UP: THE ONLY 15 MINUTES PER MONTH YOU NEED TO DEVOTE TO WEALTH

If you have successfully implemented DCA, you shouldn't be obsessively checking your portfolio. Remember the shocking truth from Chapter 5? Checking daily guarantees you'll lose money—not financially, but emotionally, leading you to make rash decisions.

Instead, we adopt the disciplined, minimalist approach of the Quarterly Check-Up.

You only need 15 minutes every three months to perform essential maintenance. Think of this as the oil change for your wealth machine.

1. Review Your Performance (The Benchmark Test)

When you look at your account statement, don't focus on the total dollar value (which will be volatile). Focus on the percentage return.

Then, compare your return to the benchmark. Since the S&P 500 (ticker VOO or SPY) is the general market average, that's your benchmark.

If your portfolio returned 7% and the S&P 500 returned 8%, you performed slightly worse than the market. That's okay, but it confirms that your heavily weighted index funds are doing the heavy lifting, and maybe your individual stock picks aren't booming.

If your portfolio returned 10% and the S&P 500 returned 8%, congratulations—you're outperforming the market!

The key takeaway here is not to beat yourself up over short-term returns but to verify that your portfolio is functioning. If you are trailing the benchmark year after year, it means you likely have too much money in low-performing individual stocks or you've strayed from your core index fund strategy.

2. Rebalancing: Getting Back to the Ratios

When we started (Chapter 6), we decided on a specific allocation—say, 70% low-cost index funds and 30% individual high-growth stocks.

Over time, these weights will shift. If your high-growth stocks (the 30%) have a stellar year, they might now make up 40% of your total portfolio value.

While that sounds great, it means your portfolio is now riskier than you planned. You need to rebalance.

Rebalancing means selling assets that have performed well and using that cash to buy assets that are lagging, bringing you back to your target allocation (70/30).

Example: Your tech stocks soared, pushing your individual stock weight from 30% to 40%. You need to sell enough shares to free up capital and use that cash to buy more of your core index funds, returning the portfolio to 70/30.

This sounds counterintuitive—why sell your winners? Because rebalancing is a risk-management tool. It forces you to sell high and buy low, and it ensures that no single asset class (even a winner) takes up too much space and exposes you to unnecessary risk if that stock suddenly crashes.

—★-★-★—

WARNING: WHEN THE MARKET CRASHES, DO THIS (THE COUNTERINTUITIVE MOVE THAT MAKES YOU RICHER)

THE FINAL DISCIPLINE REQUIRED FOR THE LONG-TERM INVESTOR IS emotional control. Days, months, or perhaps a year after you start investing, the headlines will turn ugly. Financial news anchors will be panicking. Your friends will say they are "losing money." The stock market will experience a "correction" (a drop of 10% or more) or a full-blown "crash" (a drop of 20% or more).

This is inevitable. It has happened countless times in history, and it will happen again. Your greatest challenge as an investor is not picking the right stocks; it's managing your own gut reaction during these moments of panic.

The biggest mistake a beginner investor can make is selling assets when the market crashes.

Selling during a crash guarantees you lock in a loss. Until you sell, the drop is just a number on a screen. It's temporary. Historically, the market has always recovered and gone on to reach new highs—if you wait it out.

But for the young investor, a crash isn't just something to endure; it's a golden opportunity.

Crashes are Massive Clearance Sales

Imagine your favorite store suddenly put every single item—including the brand-new console, the top-of-the-line sneakers, and the new phone—on a 20% to 50% discount. That's what a market crash is. It's a chance to buy shares of Apple, Google, and the entire US economy at a price you will likely never see again.

When you are young and investing for 40+ years, market drops are your best friend. They allow your small, consistent DCA contributions to buy more shares for the same price.

YOUR CRASH ACTION CHECKLIST (DAY 7: THE DISCIPLINE DAY)

1. Do Not Panic. Seriously, do not check your portfolio every five minutes. The money you invested is earmarked for the distant future (college, car, retirement). It doesn't matter what happens in the next six months.

2. Do Not Stop Your DCA. The single most important action during a crash is maintaining your automatic contributions. If you stop contributing, you miss the crucial chance to buy low.

3. If Possible, Increase Your Contributions. If you have extra cash in your savings account or got a bonus from work, dump a little more than usual into your core index funds. This is the moment to be "fearful when others are greedy, and greedy when others are fearful," as the legendary investor Warren Buffett advises.

4. Revisit Your Thesis. Did the company you bought (like Netflix or Microsoft) fundamentally change during the crash? Probably not. The economy just got scared. If the company is still well-managed and has great products, hold tight.

By staying invested, automating your process, and viewing crashes as opportunities, you ensure that you are riding the long-term upward trajectory of the global economy. You are no longer managing stocks; you are managing your behavior, and that is the true secret to long-term wealth. The execution phase is complete, and your money is now moving without you lifting a finger.

DAY 4: THE FRACTIONAL SHARE POWER-UP: HOW TO BUY GOOGLE STOCK EVEN IF YOU ONLY HAVE $10

CONGRATULATIONS! YOU'VE DONE THE FOUNDATIONAL WORK. You have your account set up, your cash ready, and your strategy mapped out. Today is the day you actually buy something. This is where theory turns into reality, and you become a genuine owner.

When you first open a brokerage account with $50 or $100, the stock market can look intimidating. You quickly realize that big-name stocks—the ones everyone talks about like Amazon, Tesla, or Google—often trade for hundreds, or even thousands, of dollars per single share. If you only have $50, how can you possibly buy Google stock?

The answer is the modern investing superpower: Fractional Shares.

The Fractional Share Power-Up

In the old days, you had to buy stocks in whole units. If a share of Netflix was $500 and you only had $499, you were out of luck. This barrier kept smaller investors locked out of the best opportunities and made diversification nearly impossible.

Fractional shares changed the game. Instead of telling your broker, "I want to buy 1 full share," you tell them, "I want to spend $50 on this stock."

The brokerage platform then calculates exactly what portion of a share your $50 buys. If a share costs $100, your $50 buys you 0.5 shares. If a share costs $500, your $50 buys you 0.1 shares.

Why this matters for you:

1. Instant Diversification: You can spread a small amount of money ($50) across five different expensive companies, meaning you aren't reliant on just one stock's performance.

2. Accessibility: No stock is too expensive. You can invest in any company you want, regardless of the price tag, starting with just $1.

3. Automation: Fractional shares are essential for Dollar-Cost Averaging (which we will cover in the next section), allowing you to automatically invest a set dollar amount weekly or monthly.

When you are starting small, always ensure the platform you use offers fractional share trading.

THE TWO WAYS TO PLACE A TRADE: MARKET VS. LIMIT

When you go to buy a stock or ETF, your broker will ask you what type of "order" you want to place. This sounds complicated, but there are only two main types you need to know about.

1. The Market Order (The Quick Purchase)

A Market Order is the fastest, simplest way to buy a stock. When you select a Market Order, you are telling the broker: "Buy this stock for me right now, whatever the current market price is."

Imagine you are ordering a fast-food burger. You accept the price on the menu and expect to get it immediately.

Pros: Execution is nearly instant. If the market is open, your trade will almost always go through immediately at the prevailing price.

Cons: Because stock prices fluctuate constantly (sometimes in seconds), the exact price you pay might be slightly higher or lower than the price you saw when you clicked 'Buy.' This is usually negligible for index funds, but important to know.

When to use it: Market orders are excellent for beginner investors, especially when buying highly liquid assets like S&P 500 Index Funds (Vanguard VOO or Fidelity FXAIX) where the price is stable and the goal is just to get invested quickly.

2. The Limit Order (The Sniper Strategy)

A Limit Order is a conditional purchase. When you select a Limit Order, you are telling the broker: "Buy this stock for me, but only if the price drops to X or below." You set a specific maximum price you are willing to pay.

Imagine you are waiting for a new video game console to drop in price. You will only buy it if it hits $399.

Pros: You control the maximum price you pay. If you think a stock is currently overpriced but want to snag it if it dips, this is how you do it.

Cons: Your order might never be filled. If the stock never hits your limit price, you won't own it, and you will miss out on any subsequent growth. Limit Orders also usually expire (e.g., they might only last for the day or 30 days).

When to use it: Limit orders are generally used by more active traders or if you are specifically trying to buy individual stocks during a major market dip and want to ensure you get a good deal.

Day 4 Execution Checklist: Your First Fractional Purchase

Since you are a beginner focused on long-term wealth, the simplest and most recommended approach is the Market Order using Fractional Shares.

Follow these steps on your chosen brokerage app (this process is nearly identical across platforms like Fidelity, Schwab, or Robinhood):

Step 1: Search for the Ticker

Locate the index fund or stock you decided on in Day 2 or Day 3 (e.g., VTI for the total US stock market). Type the three or four-letter ticker symbol into the search bar.

Step 2: Click 'Trade' or 'Buy'

You will be taken to the order screen for that security.

Step 3: Select the Purchase Method

This is the most critical step for new investors. You will usually have two choices:

A) Buy by Shares (traditional, full-share buying)

B) Buy by Dollar Amount (fractional share buying)

Choose 'Buy by Dollar Amount.'

Step 4: Select the Order Type

Choose 'Market Order' for instant execution. (If you chose a Limit Order, you would now enter the specific maximum price you are willing to pay per share.)

Step 5: Enter the Amount

Input the exact dollar amount you wish to invest (e.g., $75). Remember that this money must already be transferred into your brokerage cash account.

Step 6: Review the Order

The platform will show you a confirmation screen. It will read something like this:

Security: VTI

Order Type: Market Order

Amount: $75.00

Estimated Shares Purchased: 0.29 Shares (This is the fractional piece)

Step 7: Confirm the Order

Click 'Place Order' or 'Submit Trade.'

Congratulations! You are now officially a part-owner of the thousands of companies represented by that index fund or the specific company stock you selected. You have moved from a consumer of these great companies to an owner, entitled to their growth and profits.

You will see the cash disappear from your account and the asset (the fractional share) appear in your portfolio within a few moments. Do not worry about the specific price it executed at—the whole point of long-term investing is that those tiny fluctuations are meaningless over 10 or 20 years.

THE DOLLAR-COST AVERAGING MACHINE™: YOUR AUTO-PILOT STRATEGY THAT DEFEATS MARKET ANXIETY

You are young, which means you are intelligent enough to realize that trying to time the market—that is, trying to guess the absolute bottom price to buy or the absolute top price to sell—is a fool's errand. Wall Street veterans with decades of experience and supercomputers cannot reliably do it. What makes you think you can?

The pursuit of perfect timing is the single greatest cause of financial anxiety, fear, and bad decisions for new investors. It forces you to constantly check stock prices, stressing about whether you should have bought yesterday or waited until tomorrow. This is where the Dollar-Cost Averaging Machine (DCA) comes in. DCA is your robotic financial assistant, designed to eliminate emotion and guarantee you take advantage of every market fluctuation automatically.

What is Dollar-Cost Averaging? It is the straightforward strategy of investing a fixed dollar amount on a regular, consistent schedule, regardless of the share price.

For example, instead of saving up $1,000 and dumping it all into the market on one specific day, you commit to investing $50 every week, or perhaps $25 every

THE BRILLIANT MATH BEHIND DCA

THE TRUE GENIUS OF DCA IS THAT IT FORCES YOU TO BUY MORE shares when the market is down and fewer shares when the market is up. Over time, this mechanism ensures your average cost per share is lower than if you had tried to guess the market's movements.

Let's look at a simple scenario using a fictional index fund (Ticker: INVEST).

Month 1: You invest $100. INVEST is $10 per share. You buy 10 shares.

Month 2: The market drops (oh no!). INVEST is $5 per share. You still invest $100. You buy 20 shares.

Month 3: The market recovers. INVEST is back to $10 per share. You invest $100. You buy 10 shares.

Total invested: $300.

Total shares owned: 40 shares.

Your average cost per share: $300 / 40 shares = $7.50 per share.

Notice that even though the stock ended the three months at $10 per share (the same price it started), your average cost is only $7.50. You automatically bought the dip in Month 2 without even thinking about it, allowing you to accumulate more shares for less money.

YOUR AUTO-PILOT STRATEGY THAT DEFEATS ANXIETY

FOR A YOUNG INVESTOR FOCUSED ON LONG-TERM WEALTH, THE PSYchological benefit of DCA is arguably more valuable than the mathematical benefit.

1. It Defeats Panic and FOMO: DCA removes the need to worry about market drops. When prices fall, instead of panicking, you know that your

next scheduled investment will simply purchase more shares at a discount. The market crash is no longer a disaster; it is a sale.

2. It Enforces Consistency: Your job as an investor is simply to make your contribution. Once you set up the routine—whether it's $25 every two weeks or $100 on the 1st of every month—you eliminate the stress of decision-making. Consistency is the engine of compounding, and DCA makes consistency mandatory.

3. It Works with Real Life: As a teen, your income is likely sporadic or comes in small, frequent chunks (gigs, allowance, part-time work). DCA is perfectly suited to this reality. You don't have to wait until you have a huge lump sum; you can start with tiny amounts immediately.

SETTING UP THE DCA MACHINE™

MODERN BROKERAGE PLATFORMS, DESIGNED FOR USERS LIKE YOU, make implementing DCA incredibly easy. This is Day 4 of your 7-Day Wealth Launchpad, and it's time to automate the process so you never miss a contribution.

Step 1: Determine Your Investment Frequency and Amount.

Look at your cash flow funnel (Chapter 2). If you earn $100 every two weeks, commit to automatically moving $25 of that directly into your investment account. Consistency is more important than the amount.

Step 2: Set Up Recurring Deposits.

Log into your brokerage account (Fidelity, Schwab, etc.). Navigate to the funding or transfer section. You will find an option to set up a recurring deposit from your linked bank account. Set the amount ($25) and the frequency (bi-weekly or monthly).

Step 3: Set Up Recurring Purchases (Auto-Buy).

Once the money is in the brokerage account, you need the brokerage to buy the assets you selected on Day 2 and Day 3. For your core index funds (the 80% safety net), look for the "Automated Investing" or "Recurring Trade" feature.

Instruct the platform to automatically purchase the fractional shares of your chosen index fund (like VTI or ITOT) every time the funds hit the account.

Once these two automated tasks are linked, your DCA Machine™ is fully operational.

Every payday, $25 automatically moves from your bank, and a few hours later, $25 worth of index fund shares are automatically purchased. You have just outsourced the hardest part of investing—the emotional decision-making—to a robot.

Your only responsibility now is to ensure the money is in your bank account on the scheduled date and to occasionally check, every few months, that the machine is running smoothly. DCA removes the guesswork, harnesses the power of consistency, and ensures that when the market drops, you are the lucky one who buys at a bargain.

THE QUARTERLY PORTFOLIO CHECK-UP: THE ONLY 15 MINUTES PER MONTH YOU NEED TO DEVOTE TO WEALTH

If you've done everything outlined in the past six days—set up your automation, created your initial allocation, and funded your account—the hardest part is over. Now comes the biggest challenge for new investors: doing absolutely nothing.

The dirty secret of successful long-term investing is that it is overwhelmingly passive. You should spend more time learning about the companies you own (Chapter 5) than actually tinkering with your portfolio.

Why? Because obsessive checking is the number one cause of bad investment decisions.

Your brokerage app or website should be treated like a highly secure bank vault—you visit when you need to make a deposit or perform essential maintenance, but you don't hang out there just to stare at the digits. When the market drops 5% (and it will), seeing that red number every hour triggers panic. Panic leads to selling low, which guarantees a loss.

Your goal is to become a disciplined farmer, not an anxious gambler.

The maximum amount of time you need to devote to your wealth management is 15 minutes per quarter (every three months). If you feel compelled to check more often, make it once a month, but no more. This check-up is strictly for maintenance and assessment, not emotional trading.

READING YOUR QUARTERLY REPORT LIKE A PRO

When your brokerage statement hits your inbox, it looks like a government tax form written in an ancient, confusing language. Don't worry. 95% of the information is just legal paperwork or accounting details you can ignore.

You are interested in two main figures:

1. Total Portfolio Value: This is the total dollar amount of everything you own. Track this number and watch it grow (slowly, at first, then rapidly thanks to compounding).

2. Total Return Since Inception: This shows how much money you've made as a percentage since you first started investing. This is the true measure of your progress.

Ignore the daily price changes of individual stocks. Focus on the overall health of the forest, not the occasional wilted leaf. If the market is down for a quarter, that's fine; it means your next automated deposit buys assets at a discount. If the market is up, that's great; you are wealthier.

The key is consistency. As long as you are depositing money on schedule, you are winning.

The Rebalancing Imperative: Keeping Your Portfolio Ratio in Check

Remember when we designed your starter portfolio? We created an allocation plan, perhaps the 70/30 split:

70% Index Funds (The Safe Foundation)

30% Individual Stocks (The Aggressive Growth Drivers)

Over time, this ratio is going to drift. Why? Because the investments grow at different speeds.

Imagine your individual stocks have a phenomenal year and shoot up 40%, while your index funds grow a respectable 10%. Your initial $1,000 portfolio (with $700 in index funds and $300 in stocks) might now look like this:

Index Funds: $770 (10% gain)

Individual Stocks: $420 (40% gain)

Total Portfolio: $1,190

Now, look at the percentages:

Index Funds: 64.7%

Individual Stocks: 35.3%

Your portfolio has become riskier than you planned. The individual stocks (the riskier assets) now account for a larger portion of your total wealth. This is called allocation drift.

The maintenance check-up is when you perform rebalancing.

What is Rebalancing?

Rebalancing is the process of bringing your portfolio back to its original target allocation (in this case, 70/30). It is the ultimate exercise in buying low and selling high without emotion.

There are two easy ways to rebalance:

Method 1: Direct Trade (For Larger Balances)

Since the individual stocks (35.3%) are now overweight, you would sell a portion of the stocks that have performed well and use that cash to buy more of the index funds (64.7%) until you return exactly to 70/30. This locks in the gains from the high-flyers and increases your exposure to the safer index funds, reducing overall risk.

Method 2: Directed Contributions (The Lazy Genius Method)

Since you are contributing new money every month via Dollar-Cost Averaging, you can simply stop directing new money toward the individual stocks for the next quarter or two and put 100% of your new deposits into the underweighted asset—the index funds—until the ratio naturally corrects back to 70/30. This is easier and often avoids immediate taxable events (though for most teens, taxes aren't an issue yet).

Your 15-Minute Quarterly Checklist:

1. Log in to your brokerage account.
2. Review the Total Portfolio Value and Total Return.
3. Calculate your current asset allocation percentages (Index Funds vs. Individual Stocks).
4. If the allocation has drifted by more than 5% from your original target (e.g., if you are 75/25 instead of 70/30), take action.
5. Execute a rebalancing move (either selling winners or directing new contributions to the losers).
6. Log out.
7. Go enjoy the rest of your week.

By sticking to this minimal maintenance schedule, you ensure that you are making rational, strategic decisions about risk and reward, rather than emotional ones driven by the temporary noise of the market. You have set up the machine; now let it run.

—★-★-★—

WARNING: WHEN THE MARKET CRASHES, DO THIS (THE COUNTERINTUITIVE MOVE THAT MAKES YOU RICHER)

LET'S TALK ABOUT THE ABSOLUTE CERTAINTY OF PAIN.

You've launched your portfolio, set up your Dollar-Cost Averaging (DCA) machine, and you're feeling fantastic. Your investments are humming along, maybe up 5% or 10%. Then, seemingly out of nowhere, you log into your brokerage app, and the number is red. Not just a little red—deep, terrifying crimson.

The news is screaming about a recession, a housing crisis, or a global catastrophe. Your hard-earned $1,000 portfolio might suddenly be worth $750.

Your immediate, gut reaction will be to panic. To sell everything and get out before you lose more.

If you remember only one piece of advice from this entire book, make it this: Do not panic sell. Do not stop your regular contributions.

The stock market never moves in a straight line. It is a roller coaster. There are peaks, valleys, and stomach-churning drops. These drops—which Wall Street calls bear markets, corrections, or crashes—are not just normal; they are necessary. And for a young investor like you, they are the single greatest opportunity you will ever encounter.

THE GREAT CLEARANCE SALE

WHEN THE MARKET CRASHES, THE NEWS MEDIA LOVES TO FRAME IT as catastrophic failure. But you, the smart long-term investor, should see it differently: the market is having a massive clearance sale.

Think about it logically. Did Apple suddenly stop selling iPhones? Did Microsoft stop running the internet? Did the 500 companies in your S&P 500 fund suddenly forget how to make money? No. These are still world-class companies, but now, thanks to mass panic, you can buy their ownership shares at a 20% or 30% discount.

This is the counterintuitive move that separates the millionaires from the average consumers: while everyone else is running away in fear and selling low (the definition of losing money), the savvy investor steps up and buys more.

When you are 16, 18, or 20, a stock market crash is the best gift you could ever receive. Why? Because you have decades—literally 40 to 50 years—for those assets to recover and grow. Imagine buying shares of the best companies in the world at fire-sale prices. When the market eventually recovers (and historically, it always does, usually within a few years), you will have bought massive amounts of wealth for cheap.

A LOSS IS NOT A LOSS UNTIL YOU SELL

THE BIGGEST MISTAKE A BEGINNER MAKES DURING A DOWNTURN IS confusing a paper loss with a realized loss.

When your portfolio drops from $1,000 to $750, you have only lost $250 if you hit the "Sell" button. If you do nothing, you still own the exact same number of shares. Those shares are simply priced lower today. As the market recovers, that $750 will climb back to $1,000, then $1,200, and so on.

By sticking with your plan, you let time do the heavy lifting. The volatility of today gets smoothed out by decades of compounding growth.

YOUR MARKET CRASH ACTION CHECKLIST

WHEN THE HEADLINES START SCREAMING AND YOUR PORTFOLIO DIPS below your initial investment, follow this simple, four-point checklist. Note that the best advice is typically to do absolutely nothing outside of your pre-set automation.

1. Close the App and Take a Walk

The number one goal is to remove emotion. If seeing the red numbers triggers panic, stop looking at them. Remember the research from Chapter 5: checking your portfolio daily guarantees you'll lose money because it invites emotional, irrational decision-making. You are a long-term investor; you only need to check your performance quarterly. Stop doom-scrolling your finances.

2. Confirm Your DCA is Still Running

The beauty of the Dollar-Cost Averaging Machine (from the previous section) is that it invests mechanically, without emotion. When the market drops, your automated purchase buys more shares for the same amount of money. Check your settings. If they are running, let them run! This is exactly what DCA is designed for—to take advantage of cheap prices without you having to think about it.

3. Resist the Urge to 'Pick the Bottom'

When the market is crashing, you might think, "I'll wait until it falls another 10%, then I'll buy." Don't try to time the market. Nobody—not even the most seasoned hedge fund manager—knows when the absolute bottom will occur. You will miss the rebound waiting for the perfect moment. Instead, stick to your regular, automated buying schedule. If you have extra cash reserved (that you don't need for emergencies), feel free to deploy it gradually into your core index funds.

4. Review Your Original Thesis

Ask yourself: "Did the reason I invested in this asset fundamentally change?"

If you bought a broad index fund because you believe the global economy will continue to grow over the next 40 years, has a six-month market dip changed that fundamental belief? (No.) If you invested in a gaming company because you believed its technology was superior, is that technology now suddenly inferior? (Probably not.) As long as your investment thesis holds, your job is simply to buy and hold, and ideally, buy more.

Market crashes are the true litmus test of an investor. By refusing to panic, continuing to contribute, and viewing dips as opportunities rather than disasters, you harness the chaos to build long-term wealth far faster than those who only invest when the market feels "safe." Safety, in this context, is expensive. Opportunity wears a scary mask. Embrace it.

CHAPTER EIGHT

—★-★-★—

GRADUATION DAY: UNLOCKING THE ADULT TOOLS (TAX SECRETS, RETIREMENT ACCOUNTS, AND SCALING TO $100K)

Congratulations. You have officially graduated.

If Chapters 1 through 7 were about mastering the fundamentals—learning the rules of the game, setting up your team, and executing your first play—Chapter 8 is about leveling up your gear. You are now transitioning from being a smart teen investor under custodial supervision to a young adult investor who takes command of their entire financial fortress.

This transition comes with two major unlocks: more power and more responsibility. The power is the ability to use truly specialized, highly tax-efficient financial tools (hello, Roth IRA!). The responsibility is understanding how the government looks at your money (hello, taxes!).

You've built the engine (your portfolio); now it's time to tune it for maximum speed, tax efficiency, and rapid scaling. The goal is no longer just to get started; the goal is to leverage your age advantage so effectively that you hit $100,000 before you even hit 25.

The road ahead is clear, professional, and vastly more lucrative than the path of the average adult who waited too long.

THE IRS BOOGEYMEN: HOW TO HANDLE CAPITAL GAINS TAXES SO YOU DON'T GET AUDITED BY AGE 20

If there is one topic that makes every new investor's stomach drop, it's taxes. The good news is that for most young investors, the tax situation is incredibly simple, and often, the actual taxes owed are zero.

The key is awareness. You need to know when your investing activities trigger a tax obligation, so you are never surprised, and your custodian (parent) can file correctly.

The two main taxes you need to know about right now are Capital Gains and Dividends.

1. CAPITAL GAINS TAXES: THE TAX ON SUCCESS

When you buy a stock or an ETF, you establish a "cost basis" (what you paid for it). If you sell that asset for more than you paid, you have a capital gain—a profit. The government wants a slice of that profit.

Short-Term Gains: If you buy an asset and sell it within 365 days or less, the profit is considered a short-term capital gain. This is taxed at the same rate as your normal earned income (like your job wages). This is why Chapter 5 warned you against day trading—it subjects any profit to the highest tax rate.

Long-Term Gains: If you buy an asset and hold it for more than 365 days, the profit is considered a long-term capital gain. This is the ultimate cheat code. Long-term capital gains are taxed at much lower rates than earned income, provided your total income is below certain federal thresholds. For 2024, the 0% long-term capital gains rate applies to income under roughly $47,000 for single filers. Since most young investors are nowhere near this bracket, the profit you make on smart, long-term investments is often totally tax-free.

The Lesson: Hold your investments for at least one year and one day (366 days) to ensure your gains qualify for the 0% or lowest possible tax bracket.

2. DIVIDEND TAXES: THE TAX ON FREE MONEY

REMEMBER WHEN WE TALKED ABOUT DIVIDENDS—THE SMALL CASH pay-

ments companies send you just for being an owner? These payments are considered taxable income in the year they are received, even if you automatically reinvest them.

Again, due to low income thresholds, most teen investors who receive dividends will find these payments fall below the taxable limit.

The Kiddie Tax and Custodial Accounts

Since you are under 18 (or 21 in some states), your assets are held in an UGMA or UTMA account, managed by a custodian. These accounts are governed by the "Kiddie Tax" rules, which are designed to prevent wealthy parents from sheltering huge amounts of money in their kids' names.

For most teens, the rule is simple:

The first small amount of investment income (e.g., $1,250 in 2024) is tax-free.

The second amount (up to another $1,250) is taxed at the child's rate (which is usually very low).

Income above that threshold is taxed at the parents' usually higher marginal tax rate.

Don't panic. If you are starting small, generating less than $2,500 in investment income annually (including dividends and gains from sales), your tax burden will likely be minimal, if not zero.

YOUR BROKERAGE DOES THE HEAVY LIFTING

The biggest relief is that your brokerage firm (Fidelity, Schwab, etc.) handles almost all the paperwork. They send you and the IRS a Form 1099-B (reporting sales) and a Form 1099-DIV (reporting dividends) every January.

As the beneficial owner, your job is simply to be aware of the income being generated. Your custodian then uses these forms to file your taxes. The best way to avoid the IRS Boogeyman is to keep your long-term focus, minimize unnecessary selling, and let your brokerage and custodian handle the filing logistics.

—★–★–★—

THE ROTH IRA GOLD MINE: PAYING ZERO TAXES ON YOUR FUTURE MILLION-DOLLAR FORTUNE

If the custodial account was the training field, the Roth IRA is the ultimate prize: a weapon so powerful, the government actually lets you keep all the profits tax-free, forever.

What is a Roth IRA?

IRA stands for Individual Retirement Arrangement. The Roth version is specifically structured to offer maximum benefit to young people.

Here is the one catch, and it's a big one: To contribute to a Roth IRA, you must have earned income. This means you must have a W-2 job (part-time, summer gig, babysitting, etc.) or documented 1099 income (like freelance work). Allowance and gifts do not count.

THE MAGIC OF THE ROTH: PAY TAX NOW, ENJOY TAX-FREE MILLIONS LATER

A Roth IRA is funded with after-tax dollars. This means you pay the taxes on that money now, while you are young, likely earning little, and therefore in the lowest possible tax bracket.

Once the money is in the Roth IRA, it grows, compounds, earns dividends, and gains value completely tax-free. When you turn 59 1/2 and decide to retire, you can withdraw every dollar—the original contributions and all the millions of dollars in growth—without paying a single cent of tax. Ever.

Compare this to a standard brokerage account: Every time you sell a winning stock, you pay tax. In a Roth IRA, that massive wealth accumulation is shielded.

WHY TEENS HAVE THE ULTIMATE ROTH ADVANTAGE

Imagine you contribute the maximum allowable amount to a Roth IRA for just five years between ages 16 and 21 (assuming you have earned income). Let's say that averages $5,000 per year, totalling $25,000.

If that $25,000 is invested in a broad index fund that achieves a conservative average 8% return:

By age 40, those contributions are worth over $170,000.

By age 65, those contributions are worth over $1.7 million.

Crucially, you haven't added a single penny since age 21, and that entire $1.7 million growth is tax-free. This massive head start—allowing your early dollars decades more compounding time—is an opportunity a 30-year-old simply cannot replicate.

The Rules:

1. Contribution Limit: You can only contribute up to the annual IRS limit (which is over $6,000 in recent years) OR your total earned income for that year, whichever is lower.

2. Custodial Requirement: Teens must open the Roth IRA as a custodial account (Custodial Roth IRA) with a parent or guardian, similar to the brokerage account setup.

3. Flexibility: Roth IRAs are flexible. While intended for retirement, the original contributions can usually be withdrawn penalty-free at any time for emergency use (though this is highly discouraged).

If you have earned income, your most critical priority is maximizing that Roth IRA contribution before you put a single penny extra into your standard brokerage account. You are literally buying future tax-free millions.

—★-★-★—

COLLEGE FUND SHOWDOWN: WHY YOUR STANDARD ACCOUNT MIGHT BE BETTER THAN THAT RESTRICTIVE 529 PLAN

Many young investors are saving for a defined goal: college. When money is set aside for education, two main options usually come up: the 529 Plan and the standard (UGMA/UTMA) brokerage account you already have.

The 529 Plan: The Education-Only Account

The 529 Plan is a state-sponsored savings account specifically for education costs (tuition, room and board, books).

Pros:

Tax-Free Growth: Like the Roth IRA, the money grows tax-free.

Tax-Free Withdrawal: Withdrawals are tax-free, provided they are used for qualified education expenses.

Cons:

Lack of Flexibility: If you don't go to college, get a scholarship, or decide to attend a trade school not covered by the definition, any earnings withdrawn for non-educational purposes are subject to income tax plus a 10% penalty. This penalty is the 529's killer drawback.

Financial Aid Impact: While generally better than having the money in the student's name, 529 assets can still be assessed during the financial aid calculation (though this is a rapidly changing landscape).

YOUR STANDARD BROKERAGE ACCOUNT (UGMA/UTMA)

THIS IS THE ACCOUNT YOU HAVE BEEN BUILDING THROUGHOUT THIS guide.

Pros:

Ultimate Flexibility: The funds can be used for absolutely anything: tuition, a down payment on a house, starting a business, travel, or a retirement fund. There are no penalties for changing your mind or changing your goals.

Control: Upon reaching the age of majority (usually 18 or 21), the assets transfer directly to the investor with no strings attached.

Cons:

Taxable Growth: You pay capital gains taxes on profits when you sell, and tax on dividends as they are received (though, as established, this is often 0% for young investors).

THE VERDICT FOR THE PROACTIVE INVESTOR

IF YOU ARE 16 AND ARE UNSURE IF YOU WILL ATTEND A FOUR-YEAR university, or if you suspect you might need the money for something else (like buying materials for your first business or paying cash for a car), the flexibility of the standard brokerage account often wins.

The potential tax savings of the 529 are rarely worth the enormous penalty if you choose a different path. A standard brokerage account, especially if invested in low-turnover index funds (which minimize tax events), offers maximum freedom. Financial freedom is about optionality, and the standard brokerage account offers far more options.

The Wealth Accelerator: Hitting $500,000 Before 30 By Leveraging Your New Adult Freedom

You have completed the training. You know how to research stocks, you know about diversification, you know the power of the Roth, and you understand the tax landscape. Now it's time to look forward to the moment you gain full legal control of your assets and how to scale your contributions dramatically.

THE HANDOVER: AGE OF MAJORITY

At age 18 (or 21, depending on your state and the account type), the custodial assets legally become yours. The custodian's role ends, and you take sole responsibility for managing, investing, and filing taxes on the account. This is true financial adulthood.

Three Key Levers for Exponential Growth

To move from a beginner portfolio to a $100,000 net worth (the launchpad to half a million by 30), you must pull these three levers:

1. Maximize the Roth IRA Every Single Year

This is non-negotiable. As your earned income increases through higher-paying jobs, prioritize maxing out your Roth contribution (currently $6,500-$7,000 depending on the year). That money is permanently shielded from future taxation, multiplying its value over time. If you do nothing else, maximize the Roth IRA.

2. Automate Aggressive Contributions

Once you are 18 and earning a full-time or serious part-time income, increase your 'Pay Yourself First' mandate from Chapter 2. Aim to invest 15% to 20% of every paycheck.

Example: If you earn $3,000 per month after taxes, dedicating $600 to investment ($550 to your Roth, $50 extra to your brokerage) provides the fuel the compounding engine needs to hit those major milestones fast. Consistency is far more powerful than timing the market.

3. Expand Diversification and Risk Appropriately

As your portfolio grows, you gain the stability needed to start diversifying into more advanced asset classes that match your high-growth, long-time-horizon risk tolerance:

International Exposure: Dedicate 10-20% of new capital to international funds (ETFs) to capture growth outside the US market.

Small-Cap Index Funds: These are indexes of smaller, often faster-growing companies that carry more risk but higher potential rewards.

Real Estate (The Easy Way): Look into REITs (Real Estate Investment Trusts), which are essentially companies that own portfolios of income-generating properties. You buy shares like a stock, gaining exposure to real estate without dealing with tenants.

THE $100,000 LAUNCHPAD GOAL

HITTING THE $100,000 MARK IN YOUR EARLY TO MID-TWENTIES IS the most difficult step—it requires consistent effort and significant contribution.

But once you hit $100,000, compounding takes over and does the heavy lifting. If you hit $100K by age 25, history shows that even if you never contributed another penny, that money would likely grow to over $1 million by the time you reach standard retirement age.

However, since you will continue contributing, the target of $500,000 by age 30 is absolutely achievable. That level of wealth gives you true leverage and freedom, allowing you to choose your career path based on passion, not just paycheck.

You have the knowledge, the tools, and the ultimate superpower: time. Use your first years of financial freedom wisely.

—★-★-★—

THE IRS BOOGEYMAN: HOW TO HANDLE CAPITAL GAINS TAXES SO YOU DON'T GET AUDITED BY AGE 20

CONGRATULATIONS! YOU'VE MASTERED THE ART OF MAKING MONEY while you sleep. Now, for the inevitable side effect: the government wants its cut.

The phrase "capital gains tax" sounds like something reserved for Wall Street millionaires, but if you've been investing through a taxable brokerage account (like the UGMA/UTMA you set up in Chapter 3), you need to understand two key types of income the IRS cares about.

Don't panic. For the vast majority of new teen investors, especially those focused on long-term growth and not day trading, the actual tax burden is minimal or even zero. The goal here is awareness, so you never get surprised.

The two things that trigger the tax man:

1. Dividends (The Steady Pay check)

A dividend is money a company pays out to you just for owning their stock. If you own shares of Coca-Cola, they might send you a few cents per share every quarter. This is "unearned income," and the IRS considers it taxable. Your brokerage firm automatically tracks and reports these payments.

2. Capital Gains (The Profit Margin)

A capital gain is the profit you make when you sell an investment for more than you paid for it.

You buy 10 shares of a gaming company for $500.

Six months later, you sell them for $600.

Your capital gain is $100.

That $100 gain is taxable income.

This is why we stress the difference between buying (the price goes up, but no tax is due yet) and selling (the moment you realize the profit and trigger the tax).

—★-★-★—

SHORT-TERM VS. LONG-TERM: THE ULTIMATE TAX HACK

THE GOVERNMENT REWARDS PATIENT INVESTORS. IF YOU SELL AN asset after holding it for less than one year, it is a short-term capital gain. This gain is taxed at your regular income tax rate (which might be low if you don't earn much, but could be high if you have a job).

If you sell an asset after holding it for more than one year, it is a long-term capital gain. These rates are significantly lower—often 0% for those in the lowest tax brackets. This is the ultimate financial cheat code: holding investments for the long haul dramatically reduces your tax obligation.

The Teen Tax Threshold: When You Must File

Since you are a minor, your investment income falls under special rules often referred to as the "Kiddie Tax." While the rules are complicated (and change yearly), the takeaway for beginners is simple:

You generally do not have to worry about paying taxes on investment income (dividends and capital gains) unless your unearned income crosses a specific threshold.

For most recent tax years, this threshold is around $1,250 (always check the current IRS guidance, but this is a good ballpark figure).

What this means in practice:

If your stock portfolio pays you $50 in dividends and you only sold one stock for a $50 profit (total unearned income = $100), you owe nothing and likely don't have to file a tax return related to that income.

If your dividends and realized capital gains add up to $1,500, you have crossed the threshold, and taxes are due on the amount above the threshold.

Reassurance: Why Audits Are Not Coming for Your Pokémon Card Money

You are extremely unlikely to owe significant taxes as a beginner investor for three reasons:

1. Minimal Realized Gains: The core strategy of this book is to buy and hold. You aren't selling assets every week, which means you aren't realizing capital gains. Your money is sitting in the market, growing tax-deferred.

2. Low Dividend Yields: Most of the index funds and growth stocks we recommend don't pay huge dividends, keeping that income stream low.

3. The Long-Term 0% Rate: If you do sell an asset for a profit after holding it for over a year, you are likely in the 0% long-term capital gains tax bracket if your overall income (job + investments) is low.

The Paperwork Panic Prevention Plan

The brokerage firm (Fidelity, Schwab, etc.) handles all the tracking for you. They act as the accountant for the IRS. In January, they will send out official tax documents to your custodian/parent—the most common ones being the 1099-B (for sales/capital gains) and the 1099-DIV (for dividends).

Your only job? Make sure your custodian or the adult who prepares your family's taxes receives these forms and includes them in their filing.

These forms tell the IRS exactly how much money your investments earned.

Once you turn 18 and the custodial account legally becomes yours, you take full responsibility for filing your own returns based on these 1099 forms. But by then, you'll be experienced, knowledgeable, and ready to tackle it. (We cover this in more detail in Chapter 8.)

For now, focus on the investments. The taxes will sort themselves out, especially if you stick to the long-term, buy-and-hold strategy. The best tax strategy is usually to do nothing but wait.

—★-★-★—

THE ROTH IRA GOLD MINE: PAYING ZERO TAXES ON YOUR FUTURE MILLION-DOLLAR FORTUNE

You have mastered the art of making money work for you, but now it's time to master the art of keeping it.

Every time you sell a stock in a standard brokerage account for a profit, the government wants its cut—a capital gains tax. If you buy a stock that pays dividends, those dividends are taxed as income every year. Taxes are the largest expense most wealthy people face, often taking 20%, 30%, or even more of your hard-earned profits.

But what if you could shield those profits entirely? What if you could build a million-dollar fortune where every single penny of the growth—not just the initial contribution—is 100% tax-free when you take it out?

WELCOME TO THE ROTH IRA GOLD MINE

The Roth IRA is arguably the single most powerful wealth-building vehicle available to young investors. It is an individual retirement account (IRA), meaning the money is generally meant to stay put until retirement, but the tax treatment is revolutionary.

How it works: Unlike a traditional investment account where the growth is taxed later, with a Roth IRA, you contribute money that has already been taxed (known as "after-tax dollars"). Because you pay the tax upfront, the government promises that you will never pay taxes on that money again—not on the growth, not on the dividends, and not when you withdraw the funds decades later.

THE EARNED INCOME REQUIREMENT (THE GOLDEN TICKET)

THERE IS ONE CRITICAL REQUIREMENT FOR OPENING AND FUNDING A Roth IRA: you must have earned income.

This means you must have money from a job, whether it's a W-2 summer job, 1099 freelance gig, dog walking, babysitting, or running a legitimate online store. Allowance money or birthday cash, while nice, does not count. The amount you contribute in any given year cannot exceed the amount you earned that year (and it cannot exceed the annual contribution limit set by the IRS, which is currently around $7,000).

For example, if you earned $2,500 working at the ice cream shop this summer, you can contribute up to $2,500 to a Roth IRA. If you earned $10,000, you are limited by the IRS maximum, which is higher than what most teens will earn.

Why Starting NOW is the Ultimate Cheat Code

If the Roth IRA is such a powerful tax shield, why is starting it as a teenager the biggest advantage? The answer, as always, is compounding interest and time.

Imagine two investors, both contributing $5,000 annually and both earning an average 8% return:

1. Investor A (You): Starts at age 17 and contributes for 10 years, then stops entirely. They only put in $50,000 total.

2. Investor B (Your Older Sibling): Waits until age 27 to start contributing and continues contributing $5,000 every single year until retirement (age 65). They put in $190,000 total.

Who ends up with more?

Investor A wins, and it's not even close. Because those initial $50,000 started growing tax-free 10 years earlier, Investor A's money reaches significantly more than Investor B's, despite B contributing nearly four times as much capital. Investor A might end up with over $2.5 million, while Investor B might only hit $1.8 million.

The magic is that the entire amount—the $2.5 million—is free from federal taxes upon retirement.

This makes the Roth IRA the absolute priority for every dollar you earn as a teenager, even above a regular brokerage account. Why invest money that will be taxed when you can invest money that will be tax-free?

THE FLEXIBILITY YOU NEED (IT'S NOT COMPLETELY LOCKED UP)

While the Roth IRA is primarily a retirement tool, the IRS gives you fantastic flexibility on your contributions.

Crucially, you can withdraw the principal contributions (the money you put in) at any time, for any reason, without penalty or taxes.

If you put in $5,000 and the account grows to $7,000, you can always take out the initial $5,000 you contributed if you need it for a large expense (like college tuition or an emergency). Only the $2,000 of pure growth is locked until age 59.5 (with some exceptions, like buying your first home).

This feature makes the Roth IRA an incredibly safe and efficient vehicle for young people. It allows you to build wealth with maximum tax advantages, knowing that your original capital isn't trapped if life throws you a curveball.

If you have a job and earned income, opening and funding a Roth IRA should be your immediate next step after setting up your regular custodial account. You are laying the foundation for a truly tax-free, multi-million dollar future, and you are starting decades ahead of 99% of the population.

—★-★-★—

COLLEGE FUND SHOWDOWN: WHY YOUR STANDARD ACCOUNT MIGHT BE BETTER THAN THAT RESTRICTIVE 529 PLAN

MOST FINANCIAL GURUS WILL AUTOMATICALLY TELL YOU THAT IF you are saving for college, you must use a 529 Plan. They are not wrong, but they are only telling you half the story. While 529 Plans offer an incredible tax advantage, they come with a major downside: restrictive handcuffs.

For many young investors who are unsure of their future path, or for those whose parents already have sufficient retirement funds, the standard taxable brokerage account (whether an UGMA/UTMA or an individual account) often presents a far superior solution due to its sheer flexibility.

The 529 Plan: The Good, The Bad, and The Penalty

A 529 plan is a state-sponsored investment vehicle designed to encourage saving for future education costs.

The huge benefit of the 529 is its tax treatment: all money contributed grows tax-deferred, and withdrawals are entirely tax-free, provided the money is used for qualified education expenses (tuition, fees, books, and room and board). This is a massive compounding advantage.

The downside, however, is a killer. If your student decides to skip college, join the military, attend trade school, or receives a substantial scholarship, using that 529 money for anything else results in a major penalty. The earnings portion of the withdrawal is taxed at the ordinary income rate, plus a 10% federal penalty. The government essentially restricts that capital to one purpose.

The Standard Brokerage Account: The Freedom Fund

When you invest in a standard brokerage account (often called a non-retirement, taxable account), you sacrifice the tax-free growth but gain total financial freedom.

If you save $50,000 in a standard brokerage account, you can use $30,000 for college tuition, $10,000 to buy a car upon graduation, and $10,000 to fund your startup. There are no penalties. The only tax you pay is the capital gains tax when you sell the investments for a profit, which, for most teens, is minimal due to their low tax bracket.

This flexibility is often worth the modest tax hit, especially if your goals are fluid. You are hedging against life's inevitable unpredictability.

The Financial Aid Impact Showdown

Here is where the comparison gets tricky, especially for teens using UGMA/UTMA accounts. Financial aid calculations (using the FAFSA and CSS Profile) assess different assets at different rates, determining the Expected Family Contribution (EFC).

1. 529 Plans: Generally, 529 assets owned by a parent are treated favorably. They are counted as parental assets and assessed at a maximum rate of 5.64% of the asset's value toward the EFC. This is a light impact.

2. Parent-Owned Standard Brokerage Account: If a standard taxable account is owned by the parent and earmarked for the student, it is treated identically to a 529 plan by the FAFSA—assessed at the low 5.64% rate.

3. Student-Owned Standard Brokerage Account (UGMA/UTMA): This is the critical warning. Assets held directly in the student's name, like an UGMA or UTMA account, are treated as student assets. Student assets are assessed much more aggressively, often counting up to 20% of the as-

set's value toward the EFC. This aggressive calculation can significantly reduce the student's eligibility for need-based grants and scholarships.

The bottom line? If you are saving for college and anticipate needing significant financial aid, you should avoid holding substantial investment assets (like an UGMA/UTMA) directly in the student's name.

The Verdict: Flexibility Trumps Tax Breaks (For Most Teens)

If the funds are primarily intended for college, and the student's expected EFC is low, a parent-owned 529 plan is mathematically the most efficient choice due to the tax-free withdrawals.

However, if:

A. The student is unsure if they will attend a four-year university.

B. The student is likely to receive merit scholarships that reduce the reliance on the savings.

C. The investor prioritizes full control and flexibility over the money (allowing it to be used for non-educational goals like a down payment on a house or funding a new business).

In these common scenarios, the standard brokerage account, ideally held by the parent as the owner (or the UGMA/UTMA custodian), provides the ultimate financial versatility without trapping the money behind highly restrictive rules. For a young investor, keeping all options open often outweighs the benefit of a conditional tax break.

——★–★–★——

THE WEALTH ACCELERATOR: HITTING $500,000 BEFORE 30 BY LEVERAGING YOUR NEW ADULT FREEDOM

Congratulations. You have completed the most difficult part of the wealth journey: getting started and building the discipline. The financial habits you established during your teens are now your launchpad.

When you cross the magical threshold of 18 (or 21, depending on your state's rules regarding custodial accounts), the game fundamentally changes. The 'training wheels' come off, and you become the sole, undisputed master of your financial domain. This transition is not just symbolic; it's the moment you unlock the true Wealth Accelerator.

The path to hitting $500,000 before 30 is built on leveraging two new levers: your new legal freedom and your increased income potential.

The Custodial Hand-Off: Taking the Keys to the Kingdom

If you started with a custodial account (UGMA/UTMA), pay close attention to the rules in your state. When you reach the age of majority (usually 18 or 21), your brokerage firm will initiate the transfer process.

Expect paperwork, but don't panic. The brokerage firm is legally required to transition the account from the name of the custodian (your parent/guardian) into your name. This means:

1. Full Control: You will be able to manage, trade, withdraw, and fund the account without your custodian's authorization.

2. Tax Obligation: Since the account is now fully yours, you are 100% responsible for managing capital gains and dividend taxes (see the previous section).

3. Account Type: The account usually remains a standard taxable brokerage account, but you now have the freedom to restructure your portfolio or open supplementary accounts like the powerful Roth IRA.

This freedom allows you to streamline your strategy and ensure every investment decision aligns perfectly with your individual goals.

THE CASH FLOW EXPLOSION: LEVERAGING THE WORKFORCE

As a teen, your income was likely limited to allowance, small gigs, or minimal part-time pay. As you enter your twenties, your earning potential increases exponentially, whether through summer internships, first professional jobs, or scaling your own business.

This increase in capital is the fuel for your wealth accelerator. Hitting the $500,000 mark is primarily a function of two variables: time (which you locked in early) and capital contributions.

To make the most of this phase, you must formalize your 'Pay Yourself First' mandate. When you get your first big paycheck, fight the urge to splurge immediately. Instead, calculate your investment commitment as a percentage of your total income.

The 20% Rule of Thumb: Aim to invest at least 15% to 20% of every single dollar you earn (after taxes).

If you are earning $40,000 per year post-tax, dedicating 20% means you are investing $8,000 annually, or roughly $666 per month. Combine this new contribution with the power of compounding and your teenage head start, and the $500,000 goal becomes a mathematical inevitability rather than a distant dream.

MAXIMIZE YOUR TAX SHELTERS: THE ROTH IRA MANDATE

ONCE YOU HAVE EARNED INCOME, YOUR MOST CRITICAL PRIORITY IS maximizing contributions to a Roth IRA. As detailed previously, this is the ultimate vehicle for young investors because the money grows and is withdrawn completely tax-free in retirement.

The annual contribution limit is set by the IRS and often increases slightly each year, but for most investors in their early twenties, maximizing this contribution (currently around $7,000 per year) should be the absolute foundational pillar of their investing strategy.

Why the Roth IRA is the Ultimate Accelerator: Imagine that $7,000 you invest at age 22 grows for 40 years. That single contribution could easily become $200,000 or more, and you will never owe a penny of tax on those huge gains. If you invest that same $7,000 into a regular taxable brokerage account, you will have to pay capital gains tax every time you sell. Use the tax-free magic while you can.

SCALING YOUR STRATEGY: EXPANDED DIVERSIFICATION

YOUR BEGINNER PORTFOLIO STRUCTURE (70% BROAD INDEX FUNDS, 30% individual stocks) was perfect for starting out. As your wealth grows, you should begin to expand your diversification, not just within the stock market, but across different areas.

1. Global Reach: While US markets (S&P 500) have historically performed well, it's risky to rely on a single economy. Start dedicating a portion (e.g., 10%-15% of your ETF allocation) to international index funds (ETFs tracking markets in Europe, Asia, and emerging economies). This hedges against any temporary downturns specific to the US.

2. Sector Focus: With a higher risk tolerance and more capital, you can begin to explore specialized sector ETFs. For instance, if you are bullish on renewable energy or robotics, you can allocate a small percentage (5%) to a specialized fund focusing only on that emerging field, offering higher growth potential than a general index fund.

3. Real Estate Exposure (Non-Physical): You don't need to buy a house yet, but you can add real estate exposure through Real Estate Investment Trusts (REITs). These are stocks that own income-producing real estate (like shopping malls, apartment complexes, or data centers) and are required to pay out high dividends. They provide a vital counterbalance to your pure stock exposure.

THE $500,000 BLUEPRINT IN ACTION

LET'S LOOK AT A CONSERVATIVE EXAMPLE TO SHOW HOW REALISTIC this goal is, assuming an average return of 8% (well below the S&P 500's historical average):

Scenario: Starting Balance at age 18

You start at age 18 with a modest balance of $5,000 (from your teenage investing efforts).

Your Annual Contribution: $7,000 (roughly $583 per month, which aligns with maximizing your Roth IRA and a little extra).

Target Age: 30 (12 years of compounding).

Result: By age 30, your account would be worth approximately $181,000.

Wait, that's not $500,000! Correct. The true Wealth Accelerator happens when you successfully graduate, secure a professional income, and drastically increase your contributions.

Scenario 2: The Accelerated Blueprint

Starting Balance at 18: $5,000.

Annual Contribution (Ages 18-22): $7,000/year.

Annual Contribution (Ages 23-30, leveraging higher income): $12,000/year (10% of a modest $120k salary or 15% of a $80k salary).

Result: By age 30, your account would be worth approximately $507,000.

This is the power of combining an early start with consistent, high contributions when your income allows. You used your teenage years to build the foundation, and you use your adult years to pour cement aggressively. Your early discipline, combined with the new freedom to earn and contribute more, is the only required formula for half a million dollars before you turn 30.

The key to maximizing this next decade is simple: stay automated, increase your Dollar-Cost Averaging amount whenever you get a raise or bonus, and never stop learning. You are no longer just an investor; you are a serious wealth builder.

CHAPTER NINE

YOU ARE NOW OFFICIALLY AN INVESTOR (AND WHY TIME IS THE LAST ADVANTAGE YOU'LL EVER NEED)

YOU MADE IT. SERIOUSLY, TAKE A MOMENT TO ABSORB THAT. JUST seven days ago, the world of stocks, ETFs, and capital gains might have felt like a foreign language spoken by Wall Street titans. Now, you hold the keys to that kingdom. You have moved from a financial novice—a consumer—to a strategic, goal-oriented investor. You have taken the definitive step that 90% of adults wish they had taken twenty years ago.

If there is one philosophy I hope you carry forward from this guide, it is this: investing is a marathon, not a sprint. This book was designed to provide confidence and clarity, to eliminate the fear of the unknown, and to establish a robust system. It was not a blueprint for getting rich next month. We built a foundation engineered for the next thirty years.

You now possess a clear path. You know how to track your cash flow, identify solid long-term assets, set up automated contributions using Dollar-Cost Averaging, and, most importantly, you know how to weather volatility without panicking. The hardest part—the learning and the initial setup—is over.

Your primary job now is simple: stay consistent. Keep contributing regularly, even if it's just a small amount from your side hustle or allowance.

Stick to your plan. Keep learning—read quarterly reports, pay attention to the fundamental macro trends (Chapter 5), and maintain a healthy skepticism toward any investment promising impossible, instant returns.

Never forget the core lesson from Chapter 1: Time is your single, irreplaceable competitive advantage.

You are harnessing the mathematical magic of compounding interest earlier than virtually everyone else. Every dollar you invest today has two extra decades to double, and double again, completely tax-free if you leverage accounts like the Roth IRA once you start earning sufficient income. By taking action now, you have secured the cheapest, most powerful asset available: early access to growth.

Your future self is already sending you gratitude. Every dollar you put to work now will return to you exponentially later, funding your college, your first major purchase, and eventually, your complete financial independence.

You are no longer just a teenager; you are officially an investor, a wealth builder, and an owner of the global economy. Go make your money work harder than you do.

Congratulations.